DR. ACKERMAN'S BOOK OF THE
LABRADOR RETRIEVER

LOWELL ACKERMAN DVM

BB-113

Overleaf: Yellow Labrador Retrievers owned by Juxi Burr and Sonya Ninneman.

The author has exerted every effort to ensure that medical information mentioned in this book is in accord with current recommendations and practice at the time of publication. However, in view of the ongoing advances in veterinary medicine, the reader is urged to consult with a veterinarian regarding individual health issues.

Photography by: Dennis Albert, Terry Albert, Mary Bloom, courtesy of Fleabusters, Rx for Fleas, Isabelle Francais, Lola Nichol-Liptrot, Robert Pearcy, Robert Smith, Karen Taylor, and Barry Urie.

The presentation of pet products in this book is strictly for instructive purposes only; it does not constitute an endorsement by the author, publisher, owners of dogs portrayed, or any other contributors.

t.f.h.

© 1996 by LOWELL ACKERMAN DVM

Distributed in the UNITED STATES to the Pet Trade by T.F.H. Publications, Inc., One T.F.H. Plaza, Neptune City, NJ 07753; distributed in the UNITED STATES to the Bookstore and Library Trade by National Book Network, Inc. 4720 Boston Way, Lanham MD 20706; in CANADA to the Pet Trade by H & L Pet Supplies Inc., 27 Kingston Crescent, Kitchener, Ontario N2B 2T6; Rolf C. Hagen Inc., 3225 Sartelon St. Laurent-Montreal Quebec H4R 1E8; in CANADA to the Book Trade by Vanwell Publishing Ltd., 1 Northrup Crescent, St. Catharines, Ontario L2M 6P5 ; in ENGLAND by T.F.H. Publications, PO Box 15, Waterlooville PO7 6BQ; in AUSTRALIA AND THE SOUTH PACIFIC by T.F.H. (Australia), Pty. Ltd., Box 149, Brookvale 2100 N.S.W., Australia; in NEW ZEALAND by Brooklands Aquarium Ltd. 5 McGiven Drive, New Plymouth, RD1 New Zealand; in Japan by T.F.H. Publications, Japan—Jiro Tsuda, 10-12-3 Ohjidai, Sakura, Chiba 285, Japan; in SOUTH AFRICA by Lopis (Pty) Ltd., P.O. Box 39127, Booysens, 2016, Johannesburg, South Africa. Published by T.F.H. Publications, Inc.

MANUFACTURED IN THE
UNITED STATES OF AMERICA
BY T.F.H. PUBLICATIONS, INC.

CONTENTS

DEDICATION

To my wonderful wife Susan and my three adorable children, Nadia, Rebecca, and David.

PREFACE

Keeping your Labrador Retriever healthy is the most important job that you, as an owner, can do. Whereas there are many books available that deal with breed qualities, conformation, and show characteristics, this may be the only book available dedicated entirely to the preventive health care of the Labrador Retriever. This information has been compiled from a variety of sources and assembled here to provide you with the most up-to-date advice available.

This book will take you through the important stages of selecting your pet, screening it for inherited medical and behavioral problems, meeting its nutritional needs, and seeing that it receives optimal medical care.

So, enjoy the book and use the information to keep your Labrador Retriever the healthiest it can be for a long, full, and rich life.

Lowell Ackerman DVM

Biography

D
r. Lowell Ackerman is a world-renowned veterinary clinician, author, lecturer, and radio personality. He is a Diplomate of the American College of Veterinary Dermatology and is a consultant in the fields of dermatology, nutrition, and genetics. Dr. Ackerman is the author of 34 books and over 150 book chapters and articles. He also hosts a national radio show on pet health care and moderates a site on the World Wide Web dedicated to pet health care issues (**http://www.familyinternet.com/pet/pet-vet.htm**).

BREED HISTORY

THE GENESIS OF THE MODERN LABRADOR RETRIEVER

The Labrador Retriever originates from a peninsula in North America containing the Canadian provinces of Newfoundland and Quebec. Labradors were ideal dogs for working in the local industry—fishing. Water dogs of different sorts were trained to haul the cod nets ashore, retrieve

Facing page: The natural retrieving instincts of the Labrador Retriever are still strong in the breed today. Owners, Kathy and Ted McCue.

The Labrador Retriever originated as a water dog. Today the breed retrieves in water as well as on land. Owner, Terry Albert.

items that went overboard, and otherwise earn their keep.

The fishing boats made regular trips to England, and occasionally these water dogs did as well. There they were bred to English retrievers and produced the breed we know today as the Labrador Retriever.

The name Labrador Retriever seems to have been adopted by the British. The Canadians had previously referred to the breed as St. John's water dogs. The breed was favored by the royal family and King George VI was patron of the Labrador Club at the time of his death; later, Queen Elizabeth II assumed that position.

The breed was first imported during World War I and became popular in the United States by the 1920s. The American Kennel Club recognized Labrador Retrievers as a separate breed during that period. Their popularity continued to soar. The American Kennel Club's registration statistics reveal that the Labrador Retriever remains America's most registered breed.

Retriever field trials were largely responsible for the breed's popularity in the United States. The country's leading field dog, the Labrador Retriever remains an ideal hunting companion.

MIND & BODY

**PHYSICAL AND BEHAVIORAL TRAITS
OF THE LABRADOR RETRIEVER**

The Labrador Retriever epitomizes the perfect family dog: he is kind, outgoing, and tractable. While generalizations  about dog breeds do not contribute to the training and understanding of the individual dog, a Labrador must be non-aggressive and eager to please or it simply is not a Labrador. As a

Facing page: Labrador Retrievers make excellent family dogs. Jude, a rescue dog, meets his new family member.

sporting breed, the Labrador Retriever exhibits an active mind and body: both must be exercised to keep your Labrador fit and happy.

CONFORMATION AND PHYSICAL CHARACTERISTICS

This is not a book about show dogs, so information here will not deal with the conformation of champions and how to select one. The purpose of this chapter is to provide basic information about the stature of the Labrador Retriever and qualities of its physical nature.

Clearly, beauty is in the eye of the beholder. Since standards come and standards go, measuring your dog against some imaginary yardstick does little for you or your dog. Just because your dog isn't a show champion doesn't mean that he or she is any less of a family member, and just because a dog is a champion doesn't mean that he or she is not a genetic time bomb waiting to go off.

When breeders, and those interested in showing Labrador Retrievers, are selecting dogs, they are looking for those qualities that match the breed "standard." This standard, however,

Most adult male Labrador Retrievers are between 22 and 24 inches at the withers (shoulders), and females are about one inch smaller. Owner, Pierry Kuskis.

Labrador Retrievers should be medium-sized and were never intended to be considered giants. The normal weight range for the breed is 55—80 pounds. Breeders, Eileen and Ken Grant.

is of an imaginary Labrador Retriever and it changes from time to time and from country to country. Thus, the conformation and physical characteristics that pet owners should concentrate on are somewhat different and much more practical.

Labrador Retrievers were originally bred to be medium-sized dogs, but as they were used for more and more field work, they were bred to become progressively larger. Most adult males are 22–24 inches at the withers, and bitches are about one inch smaller. The normal weight range for the breed is 55–80 pounds (25–35 kg), but a better target is about 65 pounds for females and 70 pounds for males. Larger dogs are not necessarily better dogs. Labrador Retrievers were never intended to be considered "giants" and the increased size might promote some medical problems that tend to be more common in larger dogs. There is some preliminary evidence that the larger members of the breed might be more susceptible to orthopedic disorders, such as elbow dysplasia and hip dysplasia.

COAT COLOR, CARE, AND CONDITION

All Labrador Retrievers have serviceable, water-resistant coats and are relatively easy to groom. A brief daily once-over with a flea comb and a thorough weekly brushing are about all that is required. They do shed, but not excessively. They are a double-coated breed and the brushing will help remove dead undercoat and bring a sheen to the fur. They only require baths periodically.

There are three "approved" colors of Labrador Retriever:
black, yellow and chocolate. These colors are basically governed by three sets of genes. The Agouti series determines the basic color of the hair pigment, solid black (A^s) being dominant unless another gene interferes. The B series also determines color of the coat and skin. The dominant black gene (B) produces black pigment in the hair, nose, footpads, and eyerims; the recessive chocolate gene (b) fades the color to brown. Finally, the black Extension series "extends" the black coloration or it doesn't. Normal extension is dominant (E) and allows the other genes to express themselves. The recessive form (e) doesn't allow the black pigment in the hair to be expressed (but doesn't affect the nose, footpads, and eyerims), and the result is a yellow Labrador Retriever.

The coat, equipped with a soft, water-resistant undercoat, is a distinctive feature of Labrador Retrievers. Surf's up for Bogart, a yellow Lab owned by Jim and Debbie Gardner.

Without becoming geneticists we can still appreciate how the colors occur in the breed with some basic rules. Each pup receives half of its genes from its mother and half from its father. If we forget the Agouti series of genes for a moment, the genet-

yellow in color. Since dark is dominant, a dog will be dark with either two *(EE)* or one *(Ee)* extension genes. Dogs will only be yellow if they have both recessive genes *(ee)*. One important point here. You can't tell if a dog is *EE* or *Ee* by looking;

One in every color. The three accepted colors for the Labrador Retriever are black, chocolate, and yellow.

ics of coat color are fairly simple in the Labrador Retriever. The first gene will determine if the dog will be dark (either black or chocolate) or light (yellow). This is the *E* series. Dark is the dominant trait, referred to by the capital letter *E*. A small *e* signifies yellow but is recessive; it takes two *(ee)* for the dog to be

they're both dark! This demonstrates the difference between genotype and phenotype. Genotype refers to the genetic combinations that we can't see (e.g., *EE, Ee, ee*) while phenotype refers to the products that we can see (e.g., black, chocolate, yellow). If a mating of dark Labrador Retrievers produces any yel-

Depending on the breeding source of the dog, Labradors can differ in appearance. Show dogs tend to be heavier and shorter while field dogs tend to be leaner and taller.

been inherited from each parent. And, if you breed a yellow Labrador Retriever *(ee)* to any dark Labrador Retriever *(Ee or EE)*, all the offspring will be either dark carriers *(Ee)* or yellows *(ee)*.

What about chocolates and blacks? Up until now, we've just been concerned about light and dark. Now we'll see how the dark dogs can be either black or chocolate; the genetics are identical. Not only do parents pass either a *E* or *e* to their pups, they do the same with the black gene *B*. The undiluted black color is dominant *(B)* to the chocolate color *(b)* which is recessive. Dogs that carry the genes *BB* and *Bb* are black, while those with *bb* are chocolate. Thus, a dark Labrador Retriever *(EE or Ee)* will be black if it also carries the

low pups, you can infer that both parents had to be carriers *(Ee)* since a recessive gene must have

Here are the combinations that give us our Labrador Retriever colors:

Phenotype (Color)	Genotype (Actual genetic pairing)			
Black	*EEBB*	*EEBb*	*EeBB*	*EeBb*
Yellow	*eeBB*	*eeBb*	*eebb*	
Chocolate	*EEbb*	*Eebb*		

Labrador Retrievers do well in multi-dog households. Duke (black), Ali (chocolate), and Bogart (yellow) all live together and are the best of friends. Owners, Jim and Debbie Gardner.

genes *BB* or *Bb*. With two recessive genes *(bb)*, we have a chocolate Labrador Retriever.

BEHAVIOR AND PERSONALITY OF THE ACTIVE LABRADOR RETRIEVER

Behavior and personality are two qualities which are hard to standardize within a breed. Although generalizations are difficult to make, most Labrador Retrievers are alert and people-oriented. They make great working dogs because they have the capacity to be loyal, determined, watchful, and obedient. However, it is their social nature that makes them want to work with people. This is not the breed to be tied in the backyard to serve as a watchdog. Whether the dogs are shy or vicious has something to do with their genetics, but is also determined by the socialization and training they receive.

Behavior and personality are incredibly important in dogs, and there seem to be quite evident extremes in the Labrador Retriever. Most Labrador Retrievers are friendly, stable, and

17

emotionally balanced, but some breeders have created lines that can only be described as "hyper." The earliest of the breed were bred for outdoor work, and therefore, they were not ideal housepets. Today's Labrador Retrievers seem far removed from their earliest ancestors. The ideal Labrador Retriever is neither aggressive nor hyper, but rather a loving family member with good self-esteem and acceptance of its position in the family "pack." Because the Labrador Retriever is a powerful dog and can cause much damage, it is worth spending the time when

selecting a pup to pay attention to any evidence of personality problems. It is also imperative that *all* Labrador Retrievers be obedience trained. Like any dog, they have the potential to be unruly without appropriate training; consider obedience class mandatory for your sake and that of your dog.

Although some Labrador Retrievers are happy to sleep the day away in bed or on a sofa, most enjoy having a purpose, and that makes them excellent work dogs. They need a lot of activity and, if they don't get it, may become bored and develop

The Labrador Retriever's versatility, adaptability, and keen sense of dedication to people's needs make the breed ideal for assisting people as guide dogs.

behavioral problems. Exercise should be regular and controlled. Do not let Labrador Retriever pups run unrestricted because it can increase their risk of developing orthopedic disorders. All Labrador Retrievers should attend obedience classes and need to learn limits to unacceptable behaviors. A well-loved and well-controlled Labrador Retriever is certain to be a valued family member.

For pet owners, there are several activities to which your Labrador Retriever is well-suited. Labrador Retrievers not only make great walking, jogging, and swimming partners, but they are also excellent community volunteers and guide dogs. Swimming is a favored pastime, but your Lab may not inherently take to water. Give him an opportunity to advance at his own pace. If you let him swim in your swimming pool, be prepared to clean the filter more often, and make sure your dog knows how to get out of the pool on his own. Never leave a dog unattended in a swimming area—he can drown! The loyal and loving

Swimming is a favorite pastime of Labrador Retrievers. If you let your Labrador swim in your swimming pool, be prepared to clean the filter more often. Owner, June Silva.

Labrador Retriever will also be your personal guard dog if properly trained; aggressiveness and viciousness do not fit into the equation.

For Labrador Retriever enthusiasts who want to get into more competitive aspects of the dog world, consider these activities: showing, obedience, field trials, hunting, guarding, and tracking.

SELECTING

**WHAT YOU NEED TO KNOW TO FIND
THE BEST LABRADOR PUPPY**

Owning the perfect Labrador Retriever rarely happens by accident. On the other hand, owning a "genetic dud" is almost always the result of an impulsive purchase and failure to do basic research. Buying this book is a major step in understanding the situation and making intelligent choices.

Facing page: Labrador Retrievers are adorable and irresistible, making it difficult to choose just one. Give much time and thought to your purchase and never buy on impulse.

20

SOURCES

Recently, a large survey was done to determine whether there were more problems seen in animals adopted from pet stores, breeders, private owners, or animal shelters. Somewhat surprisingly, there didn't appear to be any major difference in total

Responsible breeders take the time to socialize and care for their puppies properly. This three-week-old Lab puppy is giving his first kiss. Owner, Emily Magnani.

number of problems seen from these sources. What was different were the kinds of problems seen in each source. Thus, you can't rely on any one source

because there are no standards by which judgments can be made. Most veterinarians will recommend that you select a "good breeder," but there is no way to identify such an individual. A breeder of champion show dogs may also be a breeder of genetic defects.

The best approach is to select a pup from a source that regularly performs genetic screening and has documentation to prove it. If you are intending to be a pet owner, don't worry about whether your pup is of show quality. A mark here or there that might disqualify the pup as a show winner has absolutely no impact on its ability to be a loving and healthy pet. Also, the vast majority of dogs will be neutered and not used for breeding anyway. Concentrate on the things that are important.

MEDICAL SCREENING

Whether you are dealing with a breeder, a breed rescue group, a shelter, or a pet store, your approach should be the same. You want to identify a Labrador Retriever that you can live with and screen it for medical and behavioral problems before you make it a permanent family member. If the source you select has not done the important testing needed, make sure they will offer you a health/temperament guarantee before you remove the dog from the premises to have the work done yourself. If this is not acceptable, or they are offering an exchange-only policy, keep moving; this isn't the right place for you to get a dog. As soon as you purchase a Labrador Retriever, pup or adult, go to your veterinarian for a thorough evaluation and testing.

Pedigree analysis is best left to true enthusiasts, but there are some things that you can do even as a novice. Inbreeding is to be discouraged, so check out your four or five generation pedigree and look for names that appear repeatedly. Most beeders linebreed, which is acceptable, so you may see the same *prefix* many times but not the same actual dog or bitch. Reputable breeders will usually not allow inbreeding at least three generations back in the puppy's pedigree. Also, ask the breeder to provide registration numbers

If possible, it is a good idea to see the dam of the puppy you are considering. Puppies should remain with their mother until seven to nine weeks of age.

on all ancestors in the pedigree for which testing was done through the OFA (Orthopedic Foundation for Animals) and CERF (Canine Eye Registration Foundation). If there are a lot of gaps, the breeder has some explaining to do.

The screening procedure is easier if you select an older dog. Animals can be registered for hips and elbows as young as two years of age by the Orthopedic Foundation for Animals and by one year of age by The Institute for Genetic Disease Control in Animals (GDC). GDC also administers the Wind-Morgan Pro-

gram that screens Labs for orthopedic disorders of the hips, elbows, and hocks. This is your insurance against hip dysplasia, osteochondrosis, and elbow dysplasia later in life. A verbal testimonial that they've never heard of the condition in their lines is not adequate and probably means they really don't know if they have a problem—move along.

Evaluation is somewhat more complicated in the Labrador Retriever puppy. The PennHip™ procedure can determine the risk for developing hip dysplasia in pups as young as 16 weeks of

Adopting or rescuing an older Labrador Retriever is a good means of acquiring a lovable family pet. Here's a parade of rescued Labrador Retrievers with their proud new owners.

age. For pups younger than that, you should request copies of OFA or GDC registration for both parents. If the parents haven't both been registered, their hip and elbow status should be considered unknown and questionable.

All Labrador Retrievers, regardless of age, should be screened for evidence of von Willebrand's disease. This can be accomplished with a simple blood test. The

For pups younger than 16 weeks of age, you should request copies of registration for hips and elbows from the Orthopedic Foundation for Animals or the Institute for Genetic Disease Control for both of the parents.

incidence is high enough in the breed that there is no excuse for not performing the test.

For animals older than one year of age, your veterinarian will also want to take a blood sample to check for thyroid function (and perhaps liver function) in addition to von Willebrand's disease. A heartworm test, urinalysis, and evaluation of feces for internal parasites is also conducted.

Your veterinarian should also perform a very thorough ophthalmologic (eye) examination. The most common eye problems in Labrador Retrievers are cataracts, ectropion, and pro-

gressive retinal atrophy. It is best to acquire a pup whose parents have both been screened for heritable eye diseases and certified "clear" by organizations such as CERF. If this has been the case, an examination by your veterinarian is probably sufficient and referral to an ophthalmologist is only necessary if recommended by your veterinarian.

BEHAVIORAL SCREENING

Medical screening is important, but don't forget temperament. More dogs are killed each year for behavioral reasons than for all medical problems combined. Temperament testing is a valuable, although not an infallible, tool in the screening process. The reason that temperament is so important is that many dogs are eventually destroyed because they exhibit undesirable behaviors. Although not all behaviors are evident in young pups (e.g., aggression often takes many months to manifest itself), detecting anxious and fearful pups (and avoiding them) can be very important in the selection process. Traits most identifiable in the young pup include fear, excitability, low pain threshold, extreme submission, and noise sensitivity.

Pups can be evaluated for temperament as early as seven to eight weeks of age. Some behaviorists, breeders, and trainers recommend objective testing where scores are given in several different categories. Others are more casual about the process since it is only a crude indicator. In general, the evaluation takes place in three stages by someone the pup has not been exposed to. The testing is not done within 72 hours of vaccination or surgery. First, the pup is observed and handled to determine its sociability. Puppies with obvious undesirable traits such as shyness, overactivity, or uncontrollable biting may turn

out to be unsuitable. Second, the desired pup is separated from the others and then observed for how it responds when played with and called. Third, the pup should be stimulated in various ways and its responses noted. Suitable activities include lying the pup on its side, grooming it, clipping its nails, gently grasping it around the muzzle, and testing its reactions to noise. In a study conducted at the Psychology Department of Colorado State University, they also found that heart rate was a good indicator in this third stage of evaluation. Actually, they noted the resting heart rate, stimulated the pup with a loud noise, and measured how long it took the heart rate to recover to resting level. Most pups recovered within 36 seconds. Dogs that took considerably longer were more likely to be anxious.

Puppy aptitude tests (PAT) can be given in which a numerical score is given for 11 different traits, with a 1 representing the most assertive or aggressive expression of a trait and a 6 representing disinterest, independence, or inaction. The traits assessed in the PAT include social attraction to people, following, restraint, social dominance, elevation (lifting off ground by evaluator), retrieving, touch sensitivity, sound sensitivity, prey/ chase drive, stability, and energy level. Although the tests do not absolutely predict behaviors, they do tend to do well at predicting puppies that have behavioral extremes.

eases in animals. A registry is maintained for both hip dysplasia and elbow dysplasia. The ultimate purpose of OFA certification is to provide information to dog owners to assist in the selection of good breeding animals;

Who can resist these "puppy dog eyes"? Make sure that the parents of the Labrador puppy you choose have been certified free of hereditary eye diseases by the Canine Eye Registration Foundation.

ORGANIZATIONS YOU SHOULD KNOW ABOUT

The Orthopedic Foundation for Animals (OFA) is a nonprofit organization established in 1966 to collect and disseminate information concerning orthopedic diseases in animals and to establish control programs to lower the incidence of orthopedic dis-

therefore, attempts to get a dysplastic dog certified will only hurt the breed by perpetuation of the disease. For more information contact your veterinarian or the Orthopedic Foundation for Animals, 2300 Nifong Blvd., Columbia, MO 65201.

The Institute for Genetic Disease Control in Animals (GDC)

This three-week-old litter of Labrador puppies is just starting to play. Puppies learn a lot from their littermates and should remain with them until at least seven weeks of age.

is a nonprofit organization founded in 1990 which maintains an open registry for orthopedic problems but does not compete with OFA. In an open registry like GDC, owners, breeders, veterinarians, and scientists can trace the genetic history of any particular dog once that dog and close relatives have been registered. At the present time, GDC operates open registries for hip dysplasia, elbow dysplasia, and osteochondrosis. GDC is currently developing guidelines for registries of Legg-Calve-Perthes disease, craniomandibular osteopathy, and medial patellar luxation. In addition, under the auspices of GDC, the Wind-Morgan program is an open orthopedic registry created specifically for Labrador Retrievers. This certification requires evaluation of hips, elbows, and hocks; all four limbs must be evaluated. For more information, contact the Institute for Genetic Disease Control in Animals, P.O. Box 222, Davis, CA 95617.

The Canine Eye Registration Foundation (CERF) is an international organization devoted to eliminating hereditary eye diseases from purebred dogs. This organization is similar to OFA—where OFA helps eliminate diseases like hip dysplasia,

CERF helps eliminate various eye diseases. CERF is a nonprofit organization that screens and certifies purebreds as free of heritable eye diseases. Dogs are evaluated by veterinary eye specialists and findings are then submitted to CERF for documentation. The goal is to identify purebreds without heritable eye problems so they can be used for breeding. Dogs being considered for breeding programs should be screened and certified by CERF on an annual basis since not all problems are evident in puppies. For more information on CERF, write to CERF, SCC-A, Purdue University, West Lafayette, IN 47907.

Project TEACH™ (Training and Education in Animal Care and Health) is a voluntary accreditation process for those individuals selling animals to the public. It is administered by Pet Health Initiative, Inc. (PHI) and provides instruction on genetic screening as well as many other aspects of proper pet care. TEACH™-accredited sources screen animals for a variety of inherited, behavioral, and infectious conditions *before* they are sold. Project TEACH™ supports the efforts of registries such as OFA, GDC, and CERF and recommends that all animals sold be registered with the appropriate agencies. For more information on Project TEACH™, send a self-addressed stamped envelope to Pet Health Initiative, P.O. Box 12093, Scottsdale, AZ 85267-2093.

These happy, healthy young puppies are nibbling on Nylafloss®, which is actually dental floss. Do not use cotton tug toys as cotton is organic and rots—nylon does not.

FEEDING & NUTRITION

WHAT YOU MUST CONSIDER EVERY DAY TO FEED YOUR LABRADOR THROUGH HIS LIFETIME

Nutrition is one of the most important aspects of raising a healthy Labrador Retriever, and yet it is often the source of much controversy  between breeders, veterinarians, pet owners, and dog food manufacturers. However, most of these arguments have more to do with

Facing page: When selecting a food for your Labrador Retriever, make sure that it provides adequate nutrition and is appropriate for his life stage. Most importantly, make sure that it appeals to your dog! Owner, Sharon Celentano.

marketing than with science. Let's first take a look at dog foods and then determine the needs of our dog. This chapter will concentrate on feeding the pet Labrador Retriever rather than the breeding or working Labs.

COMMERCIAL DOG FOODS

Most dog foods are sold based on marketing (i.e., how to make a product appealing to owners while meeting the needs of dogs). Some foods are marketed on the basis of protein content, others on a "special" ingredient, and still others are sold because they don't contain certain ingredients (e.g., preservatives, soy). We want a dog food that specifically meets our dog's needs, is economical, and causes few, if any, problems. Most foods come in dry, semi-moist, and canned forms. Some can now be purchased frozen. The "dry" foods are the most economical, containing the least fat and the most preservatives. The canned foods are the most expensive, usually containing the most fat and the least preservatives (they're 75% water). Semi-moist foods are expensive and high in sugar content, and I do not recommend them for any dogs.

When you're selecting a commercial diet, make sure the food has been assessed by feeding trials for a specific life stage, not just by nutrient analysis. This statement is usually located not far from the ingredient label. In the United States, these trials are performed in accordance with the American Association of Feed Control Officials (AAFCO), and in Canada, by the Canadian Veterinary Medical Association. This certification is important because it has been found that dog foods currently on the market that provide only chemical analyses and calculated values, but no feeding trials, may not provide adequate nutrition. The feeding trials show that the diets meet minimal, not optimal, standards; however, they are the best tests we currently have.

PUPPY REQUIREMENTS

Soon after pups are born, and certainly within the first 24 hours, they should begin nursing from their mother. This provides them with colostrum, an antibody-rich milk that helps protect them from infection for their first few months of life. Pups should be allowed to nurse for at least six weeks before they are completely weaned from their mother. Supplemental feedings may be started as early as three weeks of age.

By two months of age, pups should be fed puppy food. They are now in an important growth phase. Nutritional deficiencies and/or imbalances during this time of life are more devastating than at any other time. Also, this is not the time to overfeed pups or provide them with "per-benefit from longer periods on these rations. Even then, Labs don't typically "fill out" until they are two to three years of age. Veterinarians would probably recommend that Labrador Retrievers remain on puppy diets until two years of age, except that puppy diets are high-calo-

Soon after pups are born, they begin nursing from their mother. They should be allowed to nurse for six weeks before weaning begins. Owner, Diane Ammerman.

formance" rations. Overfeeding Labrador Retrievers can lead to serious skeletal defects such as osteochondrosis and hip dysplasia.

Pups should be fed "growth" diets until they are 12–18 months of age. Many Labrador Retrievers do not mature until 18 months of age and therefore rie and Labs are very prone to obesity. We therefore walk a fine line between optimal feeding practices and unwanted weight gain. Pups will initially need to be fed two to three meals daily until they are 12–18 months old, then once to twice daily (preferably twice) when they are converted to adult food. Proper growth diets should be selected based on acceptable feeding trials designed for growing pups. If you can't tell by reading the label, ask your veterinarian for feeding advice.

Remember that pups need "balance" in their diets. Avoid the temptation to supplement with protein, vitamins, or minerals. Calcium supplements have been implicated as a cause of bone and cartilage deformity. Puppy diets are already heavily fortified with calcium, and supplements tend to unbalance the mineral intake. There is more than adequate proof that these supplements are responsible for many bone deformities seen in these growing dogs.

ADULT DIETS

The goal of feeding adult dogs is "maintenance." They have already done all the growing they are going to do, and are unlikely to have the digestive problems of elderly dogs. In general, dogs can do well on maintenance rations containing predominantly plant- or animal-

Most puppies should be fed "growth" diets spread out over two to three meals daily until they are 12 to 18 months of age. Be careful not to overfeed your Labrador puppy at this time as it can lead to serious skeletal defects.

based ingredients, as long as the rations have been specifically formulated to meet maintenance level requirements. This contention should be supported by studies performed by the manufacturer in accordance with AAFCO (American Association of Feed Control Officials). In Canada, these products should be certified by the Canadian Veterinary Medical Association to meet maintenance requirements.

There's nothing wrong with feeding a cereal-based diet to dogs on maintenance rations; they are the most economical. When comparing maintenance rations, it must be appreciated that these diets must meet the "minimal" requirements for confined dogs, not necessarily the optimal levels. Most dogs will benefit when fed diets containing easily-digested ingredients that provide nutrients at least slightly above minimal requirements. Typically, these foods will be intermediate in price between the most expensive super-premium diets and the cheapest generic diets. Select only those diets that have been substantiated by feeding trials to meet maintenance requirements, those that contain wholesome ingredients, and those recommended by your veterinarian.

Don't select based on price, company advertising, or total protein content.

Ideally, you want to choose a diet for your Labrador that meets his needs, is economical, and causes no apparent problems.

GERIATRIC DIETS

Labrador Retrievers are considered elderly when they are about seven years of age. There are certain changes that occur as dogs age that alter their nutritional requirements. As pets age, their metabolism slows and this must be accounted for. If maintenance rations are fed in the same amounts while metabolism is slowing, weight gain may result. Obesity is the last thing one wants to contend with in an elderly pet, since it increases the pet's risk of several other health-related problems. As pets age, most of their organs do not function as well as they did in youth. The digestive system, the liver, the pancreas, and the gallbladder are not functioning at peak effect. The intestines have more difficulty extracting all of the nutrients from the food consumed. A gradual decline in kidney function is considered a normal part of aging.

A responsible approach to geriatric nutrition is to realize that degenerative changes are a normal part of aging. Our goal is to minimize the potential damage by taking this into account while the dog is still well. If we wait until an elderly dog is ill before we change its diet, we have a much harder job.

Elderly dogs need to be treated as individuals. While some benefit from the nutrition found in "senior" diets, others might do better on the highly-digestible puppy and super-premium diets. These latter diets provide an excellent blend of digestibility and amino acid content but,

unfortunately, many contain more salt and phosphorus than the older pet really needs.

Older dogs are also more prone to developing arthritis, and therefore, it is important not to overfeed them since obesity puts added stress on the joints. For animals with joint pain, supplementing the diet with fatty acid combinations containing cis-linoleic acid, gamma-linolenic acid, and eicosapentaenoic acid can be quite beneficial.

MEDICAL CONDITIONS AND DIET

Obesity is the most common nutritional disease afflicting dogs and cats today, currently exceeding all deficiency-related diseases combined. It is quite common in the Labrador Retriever. Perhaps the pet food companies have done their jobs too well—the newer foods are probably much tastier to pets than the previous ones, and this encourages eating. Because many people leave food down all day for free-choice feeding, animals consume more and gain weight. The incidence of obesity increases with age. It is about twice as common in neutered animals than in non-neutered animals of either sex, and is more common in females than in males, up to 12 years of age. Recent studies indicate that even moderate obesity can significantly reduce both the quality and the length of an animal's life. Fortunately, it is a situation that can be remedied.

Neutered animals should be fed a nutritionally balanced, reduced-calorie diet that has been specifically formulated for the high-risk, obesity-prone animal. Weight reduction in most animals can be accomplished with a medically-supervised program of caloric restriction. This requires a genuine, long-term commitment by the pet owner to alter poor feeding habits and provide adequate exercise.

It is important to keep in mind that dietary choices can affect the development of orthopedic diseases such as hip dysplasia and osteochondrosis. When feeding a pup at risk, avoid high-calorie diets and try to feed several times a day rather than ad libitum. Sudden growth spurts can result in joint instability. Recent research has also suggested that the electrolyte balance of the diet may also play a role in the development of hip dysplasia. Rations that had more balance between the positively and negatively charged elements in the diet (e.g., sodium, potassium, chloride) were less likely to promote hip dysplasia in susceptible dogs. You should also avoid supplements of calcium, phosphorus, and vitamin D as they can interfere with normal bone and cartilage development. The fact is that calcium levels in the body are carefully regulated by hormones (such as calcitonin and parathormone) as well as vitamin D.

Supplementation disturbs this normal regulation and can cause many problems. It has also been shown that calcium supplementation can interfere with the proper absorption of zinc from the intestines. If you really feel the need to supplement your dog, select products such as eicosapentaenoic/gamma-linolenic fatty acid combinations or small amounts of vitamin C.

Diet can't prevent bloat (gastric dilatation/volvulus), but changing feeding habits can make a difference. Initially, the bloat occurs when the stomach becomes distended with swallowed air. This air is swallowed as a consequence of gulping food or water, stress, and exercising too close to mealtime. This is where we can make a difference. Divide meals and feed your pet three times daily rather than all at once. Soak dry dog food in water before feeding to decrease the tendency to gulp the food. If you want to feed dry food only, add some large clean chew toys to the feed bowl so that the dog has to "pick" to get at the food and can't gulp it. Putting the food bowl on a step-stool, so the dog doesn't have to stretch to get the food, may also be helpful. Finally, don't allow any exercise for at least one hour before and after feeding.

Fat supplements are probably the most common supplements purchased from pet supply stores. They frequently promise to add luster, gloss, and sheen to the coat, and consequently make dogs look healthy. The only fatty acid that is essential for this purpose is cis-linoleic acid, which is found in flaxseed oil, sunflower seed oil, and safflower oil. Corn oil is a suitable but less effective alternative. Most of the other oils found in retail supplements are high in saturated and monounsaturated fats and are not beneficial for shiny fur or healthy skin. For dogs with allergies, arthritis, high blood pressure (hypertension), high cholesterol, and some heart ailments, other fatty acids may be prescribed by a veterinarian. The important ingredients in these products are gamma-linolenic acid (GLA), eicosapentaenoic acid (EPA), and docosahexaenoic acid (DHA). These products have gentle and natural anti-inflammatory properties. But don't be fooled by imitations. Most retail fatty acid supplements do not contain these functional forms of the essential fatty acids—look for gamma-linolenic acid, eicosapentaenoic acid, and docosahexaenoic acid on the label.

Zinc is an important mineral when it comes to immune function and wound healing, but it has some other uses in the Labrador Retriever. Zinc administration, particularly zinc acetate, can also promote copper excretion from the body. Usually this is not necessary or even desirable, but some Labrador Retrievers have an inherited disease that causes them to store copper in their livers; the result can be chronic hepatitis. Although this copper-induced hepatitis cannot be cured, zinc supplementation can be used as a safe and effective form of therapy.

Facing page: Stainless steel bowls make great feeding dishes for your Labrador Retriever. They are sturdy and easy to clean. Owner, Julie A. Meyers.

HEALTH

PREVENTIVE MEDICINE AND HEALTH CARE FOR YOUR LABRADOR RETRIEVER

Keeping your Labrador Retriever healthy requires preventive health care. This is not only the most effective but also the least expensive way to battle illness. Good preventive care starts even before puppies are born. The dam should be well cared for, vaccinated, and free of

Facing page: Regular visits to the veterinarian are an important part of preventive health care. Your dog should receive a physical exam as well as any vaccinations and/ or treatments that are necessary. Owner, Wendy Gordon.

infections and parasites. Hopefully, both parents were screened for important genetic diseases (e.g. von Willebrands's disease), were registered with the appropriate agencies (e.g., OFA, GDC, CERF), showed no evidence of medical or behavioral problems, and were found to be good candidates for breeding. This gives the pup a good start in life. If all has been planned well, the dam will pass on to her pups a resistance to disease that will last for their first few months of life. However, the dam can also pass on parasites, infections, genetic diseases, and more.

TWO TO THREE WEEKS OF AGE

By two to three weeks of age, it is usually necessary to start pups on a regimen to control worms. Although dogs benefit from this parasite control, the primary reason for doing this is human health. After whelping, the dam often sheds large numbers of worms even if she has previously tested negative. This is because many worms lay dormant in tissues, and the stress of delivery causes a release of the parasites. Assume that all puppies potentially have worms—

Nursing provides puppies with colostrum, an antibody-rich milk that helps protect them from infection for their first few months of life.

Assume that all puppies potentially have worms. A regimen to control worms should usually be started by two to three weeks of age—for your benefit as well as that of the dog.

studies have shown that 75% do. Thus, we institute worm control early to protect the people in the house from worms, more than the pups themselves. The deworming is repeated every two to three weeks until your veterinarian feels that the condition is under control. Nursing bitches should also be treated because they often shed worms during this time. Only use products recommended by your veterinarian. Over-the-counter parasiticides have been responsible for deaths in pups.

SIX TO TWENTY WEEKS OF AGE

Most puppies are weaned from their mother at six to eight weeks of age. Weaning shouldn't be done too early so that pups have the opportunity to socialize with their littermates and dam. This is important for them to be able to interact with other dogs later in life. There is no reason to rush the weaning process unless the dam can't produce enough milk to feed the pups.

Pups are usually first examined by the veterinarian at six to eight weeks of age, which is when

Refrain from exposing your Labrador puppy to other dogs until after the second series of vaccinations. Moon meets his Golden Retriever cousin Rowdie for the first time. Owner, Connie Howard.

most vaccination schedules commence. If pups are exposed to many other dogs at this young age, veterinarians often opt for vaccinating with inactivated parvovirus at six weeks of age. When exposure isn't a factor, most veterinarians would rather wait to see the pup at eight weeks of age. At this point, they can also do a preliminary dental evaluation to see that all the puppy teeth are coming in correctly, check to see that the testicles are properly descending in males and make sure that there are no health reasons to prohibit vaccination at this time. Heart murmurs, wandering

knee-caps (luxating patellae), juvenile cataracts, and hernias are usually evident by this time.

Your veterinarian may also be able to perform temperament testing on the pup by eight weeks of age, or recommend someone to do it for you. Although temperament testing is not completely accurate, it can often predict which pups are most anxious and fearful. Some form of temperament evaluation is important because behavioral problems account for more animals being euthanized (killed) each year than all medical conditions combined.

Recently, some veterinary

hospitals have been recommending neutering pups as early as six to eight weeks of age. A study done at the University of Florida College of Veterinary Medicine over a span of more than four years concluded that there was no increase in complications when animals were neutered at less than six months of age. The evaluators also concluded that the surgery appeared to be less stressful when done in young pups.

Most vaccination schedules consist of injections being given at 6–8, 10–12, and 14–16 weeks of age. Ideally, vaccines should not be given less than two weeks apart, and three to four weeks apart seems to be optimal. Each vaccine usually consists of several different viruses (e.g., parvovirus, distemper, parainfluenza, hepatitis) combined into one injection. Coronavirus can be given as a separate vaccination according to the same schedule if pups are at risk. Some veterinarians and breeders advise another parvovirus booster at 18–20 weeks of age. A booster

Socialization with littermates is important for puppies to learn how to interact with other dogs later in life.

is given for all vaccines at one year of age, and annually thereafter. For animals at increased risk of exposure, parvovirus vaccination may be given as often as four times a year. A new vaccine for canine cough (tracheobronchitis) is squirted into the nostrils. It can be given as early as six weeks of age if pups are at risk. The leptospirosis vaccination is given in some geographic areas and likely offers protection for six to eight months. The initial series consists of three to four injections spaced two to three weeks apart, starting as early as ten weeks of age. The rabies vaccine is given as a separate injection at three months of age, repeated when the pup is one year old, then repeated every one to three years depending on local risk and government regulation.

Between 8 and 14 weeks of age, use every opportunity to expose the pup to as many people and situations as possible. This is part of the critical socialization period that will determine how good a pet your dog will become. This is not the time to abandon a puppy for eight hours while you go to work. This is also not the time to pun-

Microchip implantation is a relatively painless procedure involving the subcutaneous (under the skin) injection of an implant the size of a grain of rice.

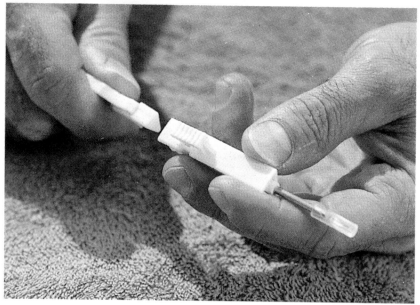

ish your dog in any way, shape, or form.

This is the time to introduce your dog to neighborhood cats, birds, and other creatures. Hold off on exposure to other dogs until after the second vaccination in the series. You don't want your new friend to pick up contagious diseases from dogs it meets in its travels before it has adequate protection. By 12 weeks of age, your pup should be ready for social outings with other dogs. Do it! It's a great way for your dog to feel comfortable around members of its own species. Walk the streets and introduce your pup to everybody you meet. Your goal should be to introduce your dog to every type of person or situation it is likely to encounter in life. Take it in cars, elevators, buses, subways, to parade grounds, parks, beaches; you want it to habituate to all environments. Expose your pup to kids, teenagers, old people, people in wheelchairs, people on bicycles, people in uniforms. The more varied the exposure, the better the socialization.

Proper identification of your

Between 8 and 14 weeks is a good time to introduce your Lab puppy to the neighbor's cat. Owner, Lisa Agresta.

pet is also important, since this minimizes the risk of theft and increases the chances that your pet will be returned to you if it is lost. There are several different options. Microchip implantation is a relatively painless procedure involving the subcutaneous injection of an implant the size of a grain of rice. This implant does not act as a beacon if your pet is missing. However, if your pet turns up at a veterinary clinic or shelter and is checked with a scanner, the chip provides information about you that can be used to quickly reunite you with your pet. This method of identification is reasonably priced, permanent in nature, and performed at most veterinary clinics. Another option is tattooing, which can be done on the inner ear or on the skin of the abdomen. Most purebreds are given a number by the associated registry (e.g., American Kennel Club, The Kennel Club, United Kennel Club, Canadian Kennel Club, etc.) that is used for identification. Alternatively, permanent numbers such as social security numbers (telephone numbers and addresses may change during the life of your pet) can be used in the tattooing process. There are several different tattoo registries maintaining lists of dogs, their tattoo codes, and their owners. Finally, identification tags and collars provide quick information but can be separated from your pet if it is lost or stolen. They work best when combined with a permanent identification system such as microchip implantation or tattooing.

FOUR TO SIX MONTHS OF AGE

At 16 weeks of age, when your pup gets the last in its series of regular induction vaccinations, ask your veterinarian about evaluating the pup for hip dysplasia with the PennHip™ technique. This helps predict the dog's risk of developing hip dysplasia as well as degenerative joint disease. Labrador Retriever breeders have done excellent jobs decreasing the incidence of hip dysplasia through routine screening and registration programs. Since anesthesia is typically required for the procedure, many veterinarians like to do the evaluation at the same time as neutering.

At this time, it is very worthwhile to perform a diagnostic test for von Willebrand's disease, an inherited disorder that causes uncontrolled bleeding. Labradors are also prone to hemophilia B and this can be tested for at the same time. A simple blood test is all that is required, but it may need to be sent to a special laboratory to have the tests performed. You will be extremely happy that you had the foresight to have this done before neutering. If your dog does have a bleeding problem, it will be necessary to take special precautions during surgery. This is also a great time to run the parvovirus antibody titer to determine how well your dog has responded to the vaccination series.

SIX TO TWELVE MONTHS OF AGE

As a general rule, neuter your animal at about six months of age unless you fully intend to breed it. As we know, neutering can be safely done at eight weeks

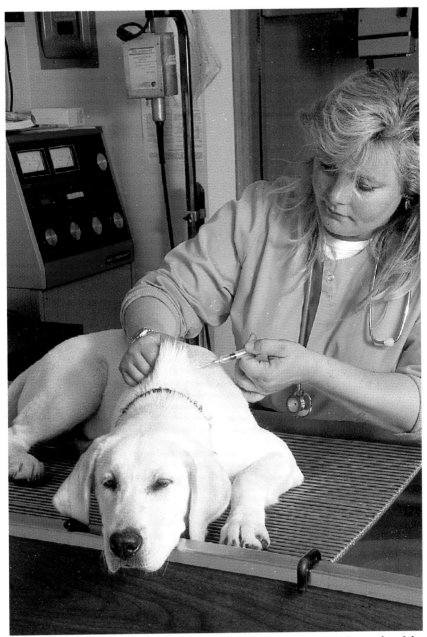

At four months of age your Labrador Retriever should receive his last set of regular induction vaccinations. After that he should visit the vet yearly for check-ups and booster vaccinations.

of age but this is still not a common practice. Neutering not only stops the possibility of pregnancy and undesirable behaviors but can prevent several health problems as well. It is a well-established fact that female pups spayed before their first heat have dramatically reduced occurrences of mammary (breast) cancer. Likewise, neutered males

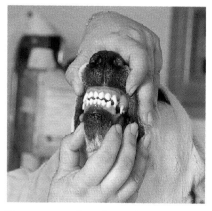

Your veterinarian should perform a dental evaluation on your Lab at six months of age to make sure that all of the permanent teeth have come in correctly. By two years of age, most vets like to begin preventive dental cleanings called "prophies."

significantly decrease their incidence of prostate disorders.

When your pet is six months of age, your veterinarian will want to take a blood sample to perform a heartworm test. If the test is negative and shows no evidence of heartworm infection, the pup will start heartworm prevention therapy. Some veterinarians are even recommending preventive therapy in younger pups. This might be a daily regimen, but newer therapies can be given on a once-a-month basis. As a bonus, most heartworm preventives also help to prevent internal parasites.

Another part of the six-month visit should be a thorough dental evaluation to make sure all the permanent teeth have correctly erupted. If they haven't, this will be the time to correct the problem. Correction should only be performed to make the animal more comfortable and to promote normal chewing. The procedures should never be used to cosmetically improve the appearance of a dog used for show purposes or breeding.

After the dental evaluation, you should start implementing home dental care. In most cases, this will consist of brushing the teeth one or more times each week and perhaps using dental rinses. It is a sad fact that 85% of dogs over four years of age have periodontal disease and "doggy breath." In fact, it is so common that most people think it is "normal." Well, it is normal—as normal as bad breath would be in people if they never brushed their teeth. Brush your dog's teeth regularly with a special toothbrush and toothpaste and you can greatly reduce the incidence of tartar buildup, bad breath, and gum disease. Provide the Puppybone™ from Nylabone® and a Gumabone® to puppies as early as eight to ten weeks. Nylabones® not only help in the proper development of the puppy's jaw and emergence of adult teeth, but help to keep the teeth clean...and the breath fresh. Better preventive care means that dogs will live longer. They'll enjoy their sunset years more if they still have their teeth. Ask your veterinarian for details on home dental care.

THE FIRST SEVEN YEARS

At one year of age, your dog should be re-examined and have boosters for all vaccines. Your veterinarian will also want to do a very thorough physical examination to look for early evidence of problems. This might include taking radiographs (x-rays) of the hips, hocks, and elbows to look for evidence of dysplastic changes. Genetic Disease Control (GDC) will certify hips, hocks, and elbows at 12 months of age; the Orthopedic Foundation for Animals won't issue certification until 24 months of age.

At 12 months of age, it's also a great time to have some blood samples analyzed to provide background information. Although few Labrador Retrievers

You should implement preventive dental care at home. Gumabones®, made of polyurethane not nylon, are good for puppies due to their softer composition.

experience clinical problems at this young age, trouble may be starting. Therefore, it is a good idea to have baseline levels of thyroid hormones (free and total), TSH (thyroid-stimulating hormone), blood cell counts, organ chemistries, and cholesterol levels. This can serve as a valuable comparison to samples collected in the future. It may also help identify those Labrador Retrievers that develop liver disease (hepatitis) due to copper accumulation.

Each year, preferably around the time of your pet's birthday, it's time for another veterinary visit. This visit is a wonderful opportunity for a thorough clinical examination rather than just for "shots." Since 85% of dogs have periodontal disease by four years of age, veterinary intervention does not seem to be as widespread as it should be. The examination should include visually inspecting the ears, eyes (a great time to start scrutinizing for progressive retinal atrophy, cataracts, etc.), mouth (don't wait for gum disease), and groin; listening (auscultation) to the lungs and heart; feeling (palpating) the lymph nodes and abdomen; and answering all of your questions about optimal health care. In addition, booster vaccinations are given, feces are checked for parasites, urine is analyzed, and blood samples may be collected for analysis. One of the tests run on the blood samples is for heartworm antigen. In areas of the country where heartworm is only present in the spring, summer, and fall (it's spread by mosquitoes), blood samples are collected and evaluated about a month prior to the mosquito season. Other routine blood tests are for blood cells (hematology), organ chemistries, thyroid levels, and electrolytes.

By two years of age, most veterinarians prefer to begin preventive dental cleanings, often referred to as "prophies." Anesthesia is required, and the veterinarian or veterinary dentist will use an ultrasonic scaler to remove plaque and tartar from above and below the gum line, then polish the teeth so that plaque has a harder time sticking to the teeth. Radiographs (x-rays) and fluoride treatments are other options. It is now known that it is plaque, not tartar, that initiates inflammation in the gums. Since scaling and root planing remove more tartar than plaque, veterinary dentists

Be sure that your Labrador always has a Nylabone® available to do his part in keeping his teeth clean.

have begun using a new technique called PerioBUD (periodontal bactericidal ultrasonic debridement). The ultrasonic treatment is quicker, disrupts more bacteria, and is less irritating to the gums. With tooth polishing to finish up the procedure, gum healing is better and owners can start home care sooner. Each dog has its own dental needs that must be addressed, but most veterinary dentists recommend prophies annually. Be sure too that your Labrador always has a Nylabone® available to do his part in keeping his teeth clean.

SENIOR LABRADOR RETRIEVERS

Labrador Retrievers are considered seniors when they reach about seven years of age. Veterinarians still usually only need to examine them once a year, but it is now important to start screening for geriatric problems. Accordingly, blood profiles, urinalysis, chest radiographs, and electrocardiograms (EKG) are recommended on an annual basis. When problems are caught early, they are much more likely to be successfully managed. This is as true in canine medicine as it is in human medicine.

MEDICAL PROBLEMS

**RECOGNIZED GENETIC CONDITIONS
SPECIFICALLY RELATED TO THE LABRADOR RETRIEVER**

M any conditions appear to be especially prominent in Labrador Retrievers. Sometimes it is possible to identify the genetic basis of a problem, but in many cases, we must be satis-  fied with merely identifying the breeds that are at risk and how the conditions can be

Facing page: Genetic diseases can be passed to Labrador Retrievers from generation to generation. It is important to be able to identify, treat, and prevent these problems in order to ensure healthy animals. Owner, Elaine Perkins.

identified, treated, and prevented. Following are some conditions that have been recognized as being common in the Labrador Retriever, but this listing is certainly not complete. Also, many genetic conditions may be common in certain breed lines, but not in the breed in general.

ACRAL LICK DERMATITIS

Few things are as frustrating to veterinarians as dealing with acral lick dermatitis (lick granuloma), a problem caused by a dog licking incessantly at a spot on its leg. A dog will start licking at a spot and before you know it, it has removed layers of skin, leaving a raw open area. The reason for this is unknown. Many theories have come and gone and we're still not positive as to why a dog would do this kind of damage to itself. Some recent research has shown that there may be some nerve deficits in dogs that develop this condition. Other research has suggested that boredom may be a precipitating cause that eventuates in a compulsive behavior.

It is important to diagnose these cases carefully since some cases may result from another disease condition, which will need to be addressed. Therefore, biopsies, microbial cultures, and

even radiographs (x-rays) are often needed to help confirm a diagnosis.

Treatment is often frustrating because, without knowing the cause, it is difficult to predict the chances of success. Most therapies use anti-inflammatory agents, but a variety of other options exist, including tranquilizers, female sex hormones, anti-anxiety drugs, and medications that reverse the effects of narcotics. More exotic treatments such as injecting cobra antivenin into the site, radiation therapy, and cryosurgery have been used in the past, but have had limited success. The newest craze is to use anti-anxiety drugs and antidepressants to treat the "compulsive" aspect of the disorder. Prevention is difficult because the ultimate cause of the problem has not been determined. Until we know more, our advice must be that affected dogs, their parents, and their siblings should not be used in breeding programs.

CATARACTS

Cataracts refer to an opacity or cloudiness on the lens, and ophthalmologists are careful to categorize them on the basis of stage, age of onset, and location. In Labrador Retrievers, cataracts can be inherited as a dominant trait (with variable expressivity), meaning that only one parent need carry the trait for pups to be affected. The cataracts in this breed have three different patterns: congenital, nuclear, and cortical with variable progression; juvenile—perinuclear and progressive,

careful ophthalmologic evaluation of both parents is warranted.

ELBOW DYSPLASIA

Elbow dysplasia doesn't refer to just one disease, but rather an entire range of disorders that affect the elbow joint. Several different processes might be in-

The Labrador Retriever's eyes should be brown in black and yellow Labradors and brown or hazel in chocolates. Any cloudiness or opacity on the lens should be brought to the attention of your veterinarian.

adult—posterior subcapsular and nonprogressive. The first form is seen with a variety of other defects such as vitreoretinal dysplasia and skeletal chondrodysplasia. Many dogs adapt well to cataracts, but cataract removal surgery is available and quite successful if needed. Affected animals and their siblings should obviously not be used for breeding, and

volved, including ununited anconeal process, fragmented medial coronoid process, osteochondritis of the medial humeral condyle, or incomplete ossification of the humeral condyle. Elbow dysplasia and osteochondrosis are disorders of young dogs, with problems usually starting between four and seven months of age. The usual manifestation is a sudden onset of lameness. In time, the continued inflammation results in arthritis in those affected joints.

Labrador Retrievers are often listed as being particularly prone to elbow dysplasia. Statistics compiled by the Orthopedic Foundation for Animals found that 15.2% of male Labrador Retrievers and 10.4% of females assessed up until December 31, 1994, have evidence of elbow dysplasia on radiographs (x-rays). Continued registration is recommended because it should be possible to completely eliminate the condition in Labrador Retrievers by conscientious breeding.

Radiographs are taken of the elbow joints and submitted to a registry for evaluation. The Orthopedic Foundation for Animals (OFA) will assign a breed registry number to those animals with normal elbows that are over 24 months of age. Abnormal elbows are reported as grade I to III, where grade III elbows have well-developed degenerative joint disease (arthritis). Normal elbows on individuals 24 months or older are assigned a breed registry number and are periodically reported to parent breed clubs. Genetic Disease Control (GDC) maintains an open registry for elbow dysplasia and assigns a registry number to those individuals with normal elbows at 12 months of age or older. Only animals with normal elbows should be used for breeding.

There is strong evidence to support the contention that osteochondrosis (OCD) of the elbow is an inherited disease, likely controlled by many genes. Preliminary research (in Labrador Retrievers) also suggests that the different forms of elbow dysplasia are inherited independently. Therefore, breeding stock should be selected from those animals without a history of osteochondrosis, preferably for several generations. Unaffected dogs producing offspring with OCD, fragmented coronoid process (FCP), or both, should not be bred again, and unaffected first-degree relatives (e.g., siblings) should not be used for breeding either.

The most likely associations made to date suggest that, other than genetics, feeding a diet high in calories, calcium, and protein also promotes the development of osteochondrosis in susceptible dogs. Also, animals that are allowed to exercise in an unregulated fashion are at increased risk, since they are more likely to sustain cartilage injuries.

The management of dogs with OCD is a matter of much debate

and controversy. Some recommend surgery to remove the damaged cartilage before permanent damage is done. Others recommend conservative therapy of rest and pain-killers. The most common drugs used are aspirin and polysulfated glycosaminoglycans. Most veterinarians agree that the use of cortisone-like compounds (corticosteroids) creates more problems than it treats in this condition. What seems clear is that some dogs will respond to conservative therapies, while others will need surgery. Surgery is often helpful if performed before there is significant joint damage.

EPILEPSY

Idiopathic epilepsy runs in families and breeding studies have shown a genetic basis for the disorder in some breeds. Because of the increasing incidence of inherited epilepsy in the Labrador Retriever, an epilepsy research database has been established at the Institute for Genetic Disease Control in Animals. In time, this should provide us with the information we need to determine how the condition is inherited in this breed.

Epilepsy is most often first seen in dogs between six months and three years of age. The condi-

tion is similar to that reported in people, and the seizures follow the same pattern. The generalized seizure usually involves certain phases. The aura is the first phase. In this phase the animal may appear restless, fearful, abnormally affectionate, or show other behavioral changes. The ictus phase, the actual seizure phase, follows the aura.

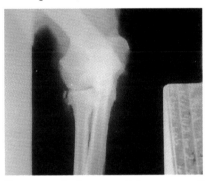

Fragmented coronoid process of the elbow, a manifestation of elbow dysplasia. Courtesy of Dr. Jack Henry.

Here the animal usually loses consciousness and its limbs become stiff. This is followed by paddling movements of the limbs. Crying, urination, defecation, and salivation may also occur. This phase may last from seconds to minutes. The final phase is post-ictus. During this phase one may see confusion, circling, blindness, or sleepiness. It may last from several minutes to a few days. There is no apparent correlation between the length of the post-ictus phase and the length or severity of the ictus phase.

The diagnosis is made by pairing a history of seizures with normal test results for other potential causes. The most common anti-seizure medication used in veterinary medicine is phenobarbital. It is very good at preventing seizures and has few side effects. The animal may have an increase in appetite and thirst, and occasionally, temporary weakness while becoming accustomed to the drug. It is important to periodically check the level of phenobarbital in the blood. This is done by taking a blood sample immediately before giving the anticonvulsant medication so the concentration of drug is measured when lowest. This blood level shows if the amount of drug given needs to be increased, decreased, or remain the same. Primidone and potassium bromide are considered options for animals that don't respond well to phenobarbital. Although complete elimination of seizure activity may not be achieved, it is still important to reduce the intensity and frequency of the seizures as much as possible. Affected animals should not be used for breeding.

GASTRIC DILATATION/ VOLVULUS

Gastric dilatation (bloat) occurs when the stomach becomes distended with air. The air gets swallowed into the stomach when susceptible dogs exercise, gulp their food/water, or are stressed. Although bloat can occur at any age, it becomes more common as susceptible dogs get older. Purebreds are three times more likely to suffer from bloat than mutts. Although Labrador Retrievers are susceptible to the condition and frequently appear in lists of "breeds most prone to bloat," recent large surveys have found that Labrador Retrievers are not as prone as other deep-chested breeds such as Great Danes, Weimaraners, Saint Bernards, Gordon Setters, Irish Setters, Boxers, and Standard Poodles.

Bloat on its own is uncomfortable, but it is the possible consequences that make it life-threatening. As the stomach fills with air, like a balloon, it can twist on itself and impede the flow of food within the stomach as well as the blood supply to the stomach and other digestive organs. This twisting (volvulus or torsion) not only makes the bloat worse, but also results in toxins being released into the bloodstream and the death of blood-deprived tissues. These events, if allowed to progress, will usually result in death in four to six hours. Approximately one-third of dogs with bloat and volvulus will die, even under appropriate hospital care.

Affected dogs will be uncomfortable, restless, depressed, and have extended abdomens. They need veterinary attention immediately or they will suffer from shock and die! There are a variety of surgical procedures to correct the abnormal positioning of the stomach and organs. Intensive medical therapy is also necessary to treat for shock, acidosis, and the effects of toxins.

Bloat can't be completely prevented, but there are some easy things to do to greatly reduce the risk. Don't leave food down for dogs to eat as they wish. Divide the day's meals into three portions and feed in the morning, afternoon, and evening. Try not to let your dog gulp its food; if necessary, add some chew toys to the bowl so he has to work around them to get the food. Add water to dry food before feeding. Have fresh, clean water available all day, but not at mealtime. Do not allow exercise for one hour before and after meals. Following this feeding advice may actually save your dog's life. In addition to this information, there have been no studies that support the contention that soy in the diet increases the risk of bloat. Soy is relatively poorly digested and can lead to flatulence, but the gas accumulation in bloat comes from swallowed air, not gas produced in the intestines.

HIP DYSPLASIA

Hip dysplasia is a genetically transmitted developmental problem of the hip joint that is common in many breeds. Dogs may be born with a "susceptibility" or "tendency" to develop hip dysplasia, but it is not a foregone conclusion that all susceptible dogs will eventually develop hip dysplasia. All dysplastic dogs are born with normal hips. The dysplastic changes begin within the first 24 months of life, although they are usually evident long before then.

It is now known that there are several factors that help determine whether a susceptible dog will ever develop hip dysplasia. These include body size, conformation, growth patterns, caloric load, and electrolyte balance in the dog food.

Based on research tabulated up to January, 1995, the Orthopedic Foundation for Animals concluded that 13.8% of the radiographs submitted from Lab-

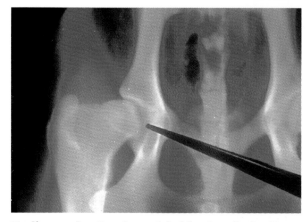

Radiograph of a dog with hip dysplasia. Note the flattened femoral head at the marker. Courtesy of Toronto Academy of Veterinary Medicine, Toronto, Canada.

cate hip dysplasia from the breed.

If you start with a pup with less risk of hip dysplasia, you can further reduce the risk by controlling its environment. Select a food with a moderate amount of protein and avoid the super premium and high-calorie diets. Also, feed your pup several times a day for defined periods (e.g., 15 minutes) rather than leaving the food down all day. Avoid all nutritional supplements, especially those that include calcium, phosphorus, and/or vitamin D. Control your pup's exercise rather than letting him run loose. Unrestricted exercise can stress the pup's joints, which are still developing.

rador Retrievers had evidence of hip dysplasia. This is hopeful news because the Labrador Retriever breeders have been able to reduce the incidence in the breed by 20–30% just through conscientious breeding.

When purchasing a Labrador Retriever pup, it is best to ensure that both parents are registered with normal hips through one of the international registries such as the Orthopedic Foundation for Animals or Genetic Disease Control. Pups over 16 weeks of age can be tested by veterinarians trained in the PennHip™ procedure, which is a way of predicting if a dog is at risk of developing hip dysplasia and arthritis. In time it should be possible to completely eradi-

If you have a dog with hip dysplasia, all is not lost. There is much variability in the clinical presentation. Some dogs with severe dysplasia experience little pain, while others that have only minor changes may be extremely sore. The main problem is that dysplastic hips promote degenerative joint disease (osteoarthritis or osteoarthrosis) which can eventually incapacitate the joint. Aspirin and other anti-inflammatory agents are suitable in the early stages of the disease; surgery is needed when the animal is in great pain, when drug therapy doesn't work adequately, or when movement is severely compromised.

HYPOTHYROIDISM

Hypothyroidism is the most commonly diagnosed endocrine (hormonal) problem in the Labrador Retriever. The disease itself refers to an insufficient amount of thyroid hormones being produced. Although there are several different potential causes, lymphocytic thyroiditis is by far the most common. Iodine deficiency and goiter are extremely rare. In lymphocytic thyroiditis, the body produces antibodies that target aspects of thyroid tissue; the process usu-

Control your Labrador puppy's exercise by walking or trotting with him on lead rather than letting him run loose. This type of unrestricted exercise can stress the pup's still-developing joints.

ally starts between one and three years of age in affected animals, but doesn't become clinically evident until later in life.

There is a great deal of misinformation about hypothyroidism. Owners often expect that an affected dog will be obese—otherwise they don't suspect it. The fact is that hypothyroidism is quite variable in its manifestations and obesity is only seen in a small percentage of cases. In most cases, affected animals appear fine until they use up most of their remaining thyroid hormone reserves. The most common manifestations, then, are lack of energy and recurrent infections. Hair loss is seen in about one-third of the cases.

You might suspect that hypothyroidism would be easy to diagnose, but it is trickier than you may think. Since there is a large reserve of thyroid hormones in the body, a test measuring only total blood levels of the hormones (T-4 and T-3) is not a very sensitive indicator of the condition. Thyroid stimulation tests are the best way to measure the functional reserve. Measuring "free" and "total" levels of the hormones or endogenous TSH (thyroid-stimulating hormone) are other approaches. Also, since we know that most

cases are due to antibodies produced in the body, screening for these autoantibodies can help identify animals at risk of developing hypothyroidism.

Because this breed is so prone to developing hypothyroidism, periodic "screening" for the disorder is warranted in many cases. Although none of the screening tests are perfect, a basic panel evaluating total T-4, free T-4, TSH, and cholesterol levels is a good start. Ideally, this would first be performed at one year of age and annually thereafter. This "screening" is practical, because none of these tests is very expensive.

Fortunately, although there may be some problems in diagnosing hypothyroidism, treatment is straightforward and relatively inexpensive. Supplementing the affected animal twice daily with thyroid hormones effectively treats the condition. In many breeds, supplementation with thyroid hormones is commonly done to help confirm the diagnosis. Animals with hypothyroidism should not be used in a breeding program, and those with circulating autoantibodies, but no actual hypothyroid disease, should also not be used for breeding.

LIVER DISEASE

Some dogs are prone to developing liver disease in association with an inherited metabolic defect which causes copper to accumulate in the liver and can lead to toxicity. This is similar to Wilson's disease in people. The Labrador Retriever is not the breed affected most often (that would be the Bedlington Terrier), but the incidence is high enough to warrant mention here. The condition is spread as a recessive trait, so both parents must be carriers if a dog is to become affected.

Affected dogs develop a slowly progressive form of liver disease. The condition is usually first recognized in young adulthood. Jaundice only develops late in the course of the disease when liver function is severely compromised.

Very recently, researchers have discovered a genetic marker for copper toxicosis that can be detected by a blood test. Although not yet widely available as a commercial test, this laboratory evaluation is an exceptionally important method for detecting carriers of the disease. Those carriers should be removed from all breeding programs, which should make it possible to completely eliminate the trait in Labrador Retrievers.

NARCOLEPSY

Narcolepsy is a sleep disorder in which animals may spontaneously fall asleep without association to tiredness. It has been documented in at least 15 breeds of dogs, but the inheritance has been studied in only three—the Labrador Retriever, Doberman Pinscher and Miniature Poodle. In the Labrador Retriever, the condition is passed along as a simple autosomal recessive trait. Thus, both parents must be carriers (yet normal) to pass the trait to the pups. Affected pups usually start to have problems between 4 and 20 weeks of age, and often have more attacks as they get excited or try to eat or sleep. The condition can be conclusively diagnosed based on food-elicited cataplexy testing, should that prove necessary. Various drugs such as yohimbine and imipramine have been used in treatment, but many Labrador Retrievers tend to have fewer attacks as they get older.

The condition can be prevented if relatives of affected pups are not used in breeding. This includes normal siblings, parents and their siblings, and grandparents and their siblings. Hopefully, we'll have a predictive test one day so that potential breeding pairs can be screened, but that is not an option at present.

OSTEOCHONDROSIS

We have known about osteochondrosis since the early '60s, and yet it receives considerably less press than hip dysplasia. Osteochondrosis is a degenerative condition of cartilage, seen in young dogs, in which the cartilage cells fail to develop properly into mature bone. This results in localized areas of thickened cartilage that are very prone to injury since they are not well attached to the underlying bone. Therefore, although the condition is called osteochondrosis, which means a degenerative condition of bone and cartilage, this is essentially a disorder affecting cartilage, not bone.

In time, when osteochondrosis causes flaps of cartilage to be exposed in the joint, inflammation results. At this time, it is referred to as osteochondritis dissecans (OCD), describing the inflammatory component and the fact that cartilage has become "dissected" and exposed. If the flap becomes dislodged, it may be referred to as a "joint mouse." In dogs, the condition affects the front legs preferentially (shoulder, elbow), but can also affect the back legs (hip, stifle, hocks) and even the vertebrae in the neck. Related conditions include ununited anconeal process and fragmented coronoid process. Elbow dysplasia is covered as its own topic.

The factors that cause osteochondrosis are many, but trauma, poor nutrition, and hereditary abnormalities have all been explored. It is suggested that feeding high-calorie, high-calcium, and high-protein diets promotes the development of osteochondrosis in susceptible dogs. Also, animals that are allowed to exercise in an unregulated fashion are at increased risk, since they are more likely to sustain cartilage injuries.

Osteochondrosis is a disorder of young dogs, with problems usually starting between four and seven months of age. In the early stages of osteochondrosis, there are usually no clinical signs or symptoms. Only when a cleft forms in the cartilage and inflammation ensues is the condition clinically evident. The usual manifestation is a sudden onset of lameness. In time, the continued inflammation results in arthritis in those affected joints.

OCD of the head of the humerus (shoulder) is often seen in pups less than seven months of age, but one-third of the cases are not detected until a year of age. The classic picture is one of lameness, and usually only one leg is involved initially. Affected

Labradors that are allowed to exercise freely off-lead are at increased risk of osteochondrosis since they are more likely to sustain cartilage injuries.

dogs can't support their weight on the leg, so they walk with shortened strides, often raising their heads as the weight is placed on the bad leg. Both front legs eventually become affected in about 50% of the cases. In time, if the problem is not addressed, the joint eventually becomes incapacitated with arthritis.

Osteochondrosis of the hind legs is much less common than OCD of the shoulder or elbow. In addition, some cases heal spontaneously which may explain in part why it is more rarely reported. Affected dogs have lameness of one or both back legs and a shortened stride on the affected leg(s). Also, the joint capsule on the affected leg(s) may be swollen. This condition (OCD of the hock or stifle) is most commonly seen in large-breed dogs, especially the Rottweiler, Labrador Retriever, and Golden Retriever.

The diagnosis of OCD is often strongly suspected when a young dog suddenly becomes painfully lame. Careful manipulation by a veterinarian can usually pinpoint the site of the problem. It is imperative that the manipulation be exact so as not to confuse elbow problems with those in the shoulder, or hip problems with those in the stifle. The opposite limb should also be carefully evaluated, even if there are no problems evident. Radiographs help confirm the diagnosis. If finances allow, it is worthwhile to take radiographs of both limbs for comparison purposes. Radiographs should also be taken of other joints on the same limb (e.g., elbow, shoulder) to evaluate for other potential sites of involvement. Because osteochondrosis is so common in the Labrador Retriever, the Institute for Genetic Disease Control in Animals (GDC) administers the Wind-Morgan Program that certifies hips, elbows, and hocks on Labrador Retrievers used for breeding.

The management of dogs with OCD is a matter of much debate and controversy. Some recommend surgery before permanent damage is done. Others recommend conservative therapy of rest, pain-killers, and safe treatments such as polysulfated glycosaminoglycans. Polysulfated glycosaminoglycan (PSGAG) is a natural product with claims of protecting and repairing cartilage. It is being used experimentally in dogs and is not yet licensed for use in this species. Usually it is given as an intramuscular injection every four days for six doses, and then ev-ery four to six weeks as needed. Each type of therapy has proponents. What seems clear is that some dogs will respond to conservative therapies, while others need surgery. Regardless of your position, prevention is the key. Therefore, breeding stock should be selected from those animals without a history of osteochondrosis, preferably for several generations.

PROGRESSIVE RETINAL ATROPHY

Progressive retinal atrophy (PRA) refers to several inherited disorders that affect the retina and result in blindness. PRA is thought to be inherited with each breed demonstrating a specific age of onset and pattern of inheritance. In the Labrador Retriever, there is a late onset of problems and the disease gene has been characterized as *prcd*. This represents a mutation in the same allelic gene. The condition is transmitted genetically as an autosomal recessive trait, meaning that both parents must be carriers.

There is progressive atrophy or degeneration of the retinal tissue. Visual impairment occurs slowly but progressively. Therefore, animals often adapt to their reduced vision until it is compromised to near blindness. Because of this, owners may not notice any visual impairment until the condition has progressed significantly.

Retinal degeneration implies that the retina was normal at birth and later developed problems. This is the subtype of PRA seen in the Labrador Retriever. Because dogs have many other well-developed senses, such as smell and hearing, their lack of sight is usually not immediately evident. The loss of vision is slow but progressive, and blindness eventually results.

The diagnosis of PRA can be made in two ways: direct visualization of the retina and electroretinography (ERG). The use of indirect ophthalmoscopy requires a great deal of training and expertise and is more commonly performed by ophthalmology specialists than general practitioners. Diagnostic changes are not usually apparent until four to six years of age. The other is a highly sensitive test, usually available only from specialists, the ERG. The procedure is painless, but usually available only from specialty centers. This instrument is sensitive enough to detect even the early onset of disease. In the Labrador Retriever, diagnostic changes are usually evident by one year of age.

Unfortunately, there is no treatment available for progressive retinal atrophy and all affected dogs eventually go blind. Identification of affected breeding animals is essential to prevent spread of the condition within the breed. Breeding animals should be examined annually by a veterinary ophthalmologist. A DNA test for PRA-affected and carrier animals has been formulated for use in the Irish Setter and can be conducted with a single blood test. Future research is necessary to create a suitable test for the form of progressive rod-cone degeneration seen in the Labrador Retriever.

VON WILLEBRAND'S DISEASE

The most commonly inherited bleeding disorder of dogs is von Willebrand's disease (vWD). The abnormal gene can be inherited from one or both parents. If both parents pass on the gene, most of the resultant pups fail to thrive and will die. In most cases, though, the pup inherits a relative lack of clotting ability which is quite variable. For instance, one dog may have 15% of the clotting factor, while another might have 60%. The higher the amount, the less likely it will be that the bleeding will be readily evident, since spontaneous bleeding is usually only seen when dogs have less than 30% of the normal level of von Willebrand clotting factor. Thus, some dogs don't get diagnosed until they are neutered or spayed, in which case they end up bleeding uncontrollably or they develop pockets of blood (hematomas) at the surgical site. In addition to the inherited form of vWD, this disorder can also be acquired in association with familial hypothyroidism. This form is usually seen in Labrador Retrievers older than five years of age.

Because the incidence appears to be on the rise, von Willebrand's disease is extremely important in the Labrador Retriever. However, there is good news. There are tests available to determine the amount of von Willebrand factor in the blood, and they are accurate and reasonably priced. Labrador Retrievers used for breeding should have normal amounts of von Willebrand factor in their blood and so should all pups that are adopted as household pets. Carriers should not be used for breeding, even if they appear clinically normal. Since hypothyroidism can be linked with von Willebrand's disease, thyroid profiles can also be a useful part of the screening procedure in older Labrador Retrievers.

OTHER CONDITIONS SEEN IN THE LABRADOR RETRIEVER

Body fold dermatitis
Carpal subluxation
Central progressive retinal atrophy
Cerebellar abiotrophy
Congenital hypotrichosis
Craniomandibular osteopathy
Cystinuria
Diabetes mellitus
Distichiasis
Ectropion
Enophthalmos
Entropion
Esophageal motility disorders
Familial reflex myoclonus
Hemophilia A
Hemophilia B
Hypertrophic osteodystrophy
Juvenile cellulitis
Mucinosis
Muscle fiber (type II) deficiency
Myotonia
Obesity
Oligodontia (missing premolars)
Polydontia (supernumerary teeth)
Portosystemic shunt
Retinal detachment
Retinal dysplasia
Seborrhea
Squamous-cell carcinoma
Vaginal edema/prolapse
Vitiligo

Facing page: It is important that Labradors used for breeding are screened for all genetic diseases both for the sake of the litter as well as that of the breed.

INFECTIONS & INFESTATIONS

HOW TO PROTECT YOUR LABRADOR RETRIEVER FROM PARASITES AND MICROBES

An important part of keeping your Labrador Retriever healthy is to prevent problems caused by parasites and microbes. Although there are a variety of drugs available that can help limit problems, prevention is always the desired option. Taking the proper precautions leads to less aggra-

Facing page: If your Labrador is itching, it could be a sign that he has fleas or some type of skin irritation. Check his coat carefully to determine the cause. Owner, Kathy Sneider.

vation, less itching, and less expense.

FLEAS

Fleas are common parasites, but not an inevitable part of every pet-owner's reality. If you take the time to understand some of the basics of flea population dynamics, control is both conceivable and practical.

Fleas have four life stages (egg, larva, pupa, adult), and each stage responds to some therapies while being resistant to others. Failing to understand this is the major reason that some people have so much trouble getting the upper hand in the battle to control fleas.

Fleas spend all their time on the host animal (in this case your dog) and only leave if physically removed by brushing, bathing, or scratching. However, the eggs that are laid on the animal are not sticky and fall to the ground to contaminate the environment. Our goal must be to remove the fleas from the animals in the house, from the house itself, and from the immediate outdoor environment. Part of our plan must also involve using different medications to get rid of the different life stages, as well as minimizing the use of potentially harmful insecticides that could be poisonous

for pets and family members.

A flea comb is a very handy device for recovering fleas from pets. The best places to comb are the tailhead, groin area, armpits, back, and neck region. Fleas collected should be dropped into a container of alcohol, which will quickly kill them before they can escape. In addition, all pets should be bathed with a cleansing shampoo (or flea shampoo) to remove fleas and eggs. This has no residual effect, however, and fleas can jump back on immediately after the bath if nothing else is done. Rather than using potent insecticidal dips and sprays, consider products containing safe pyrethrins, imidacloprid or fipronil and insect growth regulators (such as methoprene and pyripoxyfen) or insect development inhibitors (IDIs) such as lufenuron. These products are not only extremely safe, but the combination is effective against eggs, larvae, and adults. This only leaves the pupal stage to cause continued problems. Insect growth regulators can also be safely given as once-a-month oral preparations. Electronic flea collars are not to be recommended for any dogs.

Vacuuming is a good first step to cleaning up the household because it picks up about 50% of the flea eggs and stimulates flea pupae to emerge as adults, a stage when they are easier to kill with insecticides. The vacuum bag should be removed and discarded with each treatment. Household treatment can then be initiated with pyrethrins and a combination of either insect growth regulators or sodium polyborate (a borax derivative). The pyrethrins need to be reapplied every two to three weeks, but the insect growth regulators last about two to three months, and many companies guarantee sodium polyborate for a full year. Stronger insecticides, such as carbamates and organophosphates, can be used and will last three to four weeks in the household, but they are potentially toxic and offer no real advantages other than their persistence in the home environment (this is also one of their major disadvantages).

When an insecticide is combined with an insect growth regulator, flea control is most likely to be successful. The insecticide kills the adult fleas, and the insect growth regulator affects the eggs and larvae. However, insecticides kill less than 20% of flea cocoons (pupae). Because of this, new fleas may hatch in two to three weeks despite appropriate application of products. Known as the "pupal window," this is one of the most

In addition to treating your pet for fleas, treatment of the environment is essential in eradicating any infestation.

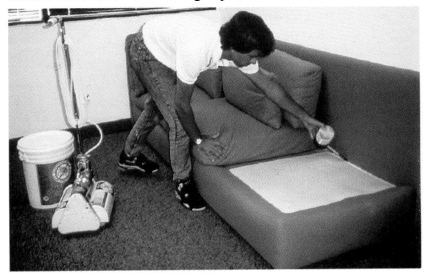

common obstacles to effective flea control. This is why a safe insecticide should be applied to the home environment two to three weeks after the initial treatment to catch the newly hatched pupae before they have a chance to lay eggs and perpetuate the flea problem.

If treatment of the outdoor environment is needed, there are several options. Pyripoxyfen, an insect growth regulator, is stable in sunlight and can be used outdoors. Sodium polyborate can be used as well, but it is important that it not be inadvertently eaten by pets. Organophosphates and carbamates are sometimes recommended for outdoor use, and it is not necessary to treat the entire property. Flea control should be directed predominantly at garden margins, porches, dog houses, garages, and other pet lounging areas. Fleas don't do well with direct exposure to sunlight, so generalized lawn treatment is not needed. Finally, microscopic worms (nematodes) are available that can be sprayed onto the lawn with a garden sprayer. The nematodes eat immature flea forms and then biodegrade without harming anything else.

Field Labrador Retrievers have a greater susceptibility to ticks given their working environment.

TICKS

Ticks are found worldwide and can cause a variety of problems including blood loss, tick paralysis, Lyme disease, "tick fever," Rocky Mountain spotted fever, and babesiosis. All are serious diseases which need to be prevented whenever possible. This is only possible by limiting our pets' exposure to ticks.

For those species of tick that dwell indoors, the eggs are laid mostly in cracks and on vertical surfaces in kennels and homes. Most species are found outside in vegetation, such as grassy meadows, woods, brush, and weeds.

Your Lab should be carefully inspected after walks through wooded areas, and any ticks should be removed promptly and carefully.

Ticks feed only on blood, but they don't actually bite. They attach to a host by sticking their harpoon-shaped mouth parts into the host's skin and sucking blood. Some ticks can increase their size 20–50 times as they feed. Ticks can often be found between the toes and in the ears, although they can appear anywhere on the host's skin surface.

A good approach to preventing ticks is to remove underbrush and leaf litter, and to thin the trees in areas where dogs are allowed. This removes the cover and food sources for small mammals that serve as hosts for ticks. Ticks must have adequate cover that provides high levels of mois-

ture and an opportunity for contact with animals. Keeping the lawn well maintained also makes ticks less likely to drop by and stay.

Because of the potential for ticks to transmit a variety of harmful diseases, dogs should be carefully inspected after walks through wooded areas, and any ticks should be removed carefully and promptly. Care should be taken not to squeeze, crush, or puncture the tick's body since exposure to the tick's body fluids may lead to the spread of any disease carried by that tick to the animal or to the person removing the tick. The tick should be disposed of in a container of alcohol or flushed down the toilet. If the site becomes infected, veterinary attention should be sought immediately. Insecticides and repellents should only be applied to pets following appropriate veterinary advice, since indiscriminate use can be dangerous. Recently, a new tick collar which contains amitraz has become available. This collar not only kills ticks but causes them to retract from the skin within two to three days. This greatly reduces the chances of ticks transmitting a variety of diseases. A spray formulation also has recently been developed and marketed. It might seem that there should be vaccines for all the diseases carried by ticks, but only a Lyme disease *(borrelia burgdorferi)* vaccination is currently available.

MANGE

Mange refers to any skin condition caused by mites. The contagious mites include ear mites, scabies mites, cheyletiella mites, and chiggers. Demodectic mange is associated with proliferation of demodex mites, but these mites are not considered contagious.

The most common causes of mange in dogs are ear mites, which are extremely contagious. The best way to avoid ear mites is to buy pups from sources that don't have problems with ear mite infestation. Pups readily acquire ear mites when kept in crowded environments in which other animals might be carriers. Treatment is effective if whole body (or systemic) therapy is used, but relapses are common when medication in the ear canal is the only approach. This is because the mites tend to crawl out of the ear canal when medications are applied. They simply feed elsewhere on the body until it is safe for them to return to the ears.

Scabies mites and cheyletiella mites are passed on by other dogs that are carrying the mites. They are "social" diseases that can be prevented by avoiding exposure of your dog to others that are infested. Scabies (sarcoptic mange) has the dubious honor of being the most itchy disease to which dogs are susceptible. Chigger mites are present in forested areas, and dogs acquire them by roaming in these areas. All types of mites can be effectively diagnosed and treated by your veterinarian should your dog happen to become infested.

HEARTWORM

Heartworm disease is caused by the worm *dirofilaria immitis* and is spread by mosquitoes. The female heartworms produce microfilariae (baby worms) that circulate in the bloodstream, waiting to be picked up by mosquitoes that pass the infection along. Dogs do not get heartworm by socializing with infected dogs; they only get infected by mosquitoes that carry the infective microfilariae. The adult heartworms grow in the dog's heart and major blood vessels, and eventually cause heart failure.

Fortunately, heartworm is easily prevented by safe oral medications that can be administered daily or on a once-a-month basis. The once-a-month preparations also help prevent many of the common intestinal parasites, such as hookworms, roundworms, and whipworms.

Prior to giving any preventive medication for heartworm, an antigen test (an immunologic test that detects heartworms) should be performed by a veterinarian since it is dangerous to give the medication to dogs that harbor the parasite. Some experts also recommend a microfilarial test just to be doubly certain. Once the test results show that the dog is free of heartworms, the preventive therapy can be commenced. The length of time the heartworm preventives must be given depends on the length of the mosquito season. In some parts of the country, dogs are on preventive therapy year round. Heartworm vaccines may soon be available, but the preventives now available are easy to administer, inexpensive, and quite safe.

INTESTINAL PARASITES

The most important internal parasites in dogs are roundworms, hookworms, tapeworms, and whipworms. Roundworms are the most common. It has been estimated that 13 trillion roundworm eggs are discharged in dog feces every day! Studies have shown that 75% of all pups carry roundworms and start shedding them by three weeks of age. People are infected by exposure to dog feces containing infective roundworm eggs, not by handling pups. Hookworms can cause a disorder known as cutaneous larva migrans in people. In dogs, they are most dangerous to puppies, since they latch onto the intestines and suck blood. They can cause anemia and even death when they are present in large numbers. The most common tapeworm is *dipylidium caninum*, which is spread by fleas. However, another tapeworm *(echinococcus multilocularis)* can cause fatal disease in people and can be spread to people from dogs. Whipworms live in the lower aspects of the intestines. Dogs get whipworms by consuming infective larvae. However, it can take another three months before they start shedding the worms in their stool, greatly complicating diagnosis. In other words, a dog can be infected by whipworms, but fecal evaluations will usually be negative until the dog starts passing the eggs three months after becoming infected.

Other parasites, such as coccidia, cryptosporidium, giardia, and flukes can also cause problems in dogs. The best way to prevent all internal parasite problems is to have pups dewormed according to your veterinarian's recommendations and to have parasite checks done on a regular basis, at least annually.

VIRAL INFECTIONS

Dogs get viral infections such as distemper, hepatitis, parvovirus, and rabies by exposure to infected animals. The key to prevention is controlled exposure to other animals and, of course, vaccination. Today's vaccines

are extremely effective, and properly vaccinated dogs are at minimal risk for contracting these diseases. However, it is still important to limit your dog's exposure to other animals that might be harboring infection. When selecting a facility for boarding or grooming, make sure the facility limits its clientele to animals that have documented vaccine histories. This is in everyone's best interest. Similarly, make sure your veterinarian has a quarantine area for infected dogs and that animals aren't admitted for surgery, boarding, grooming, or diagnostic testing without up-to-date vaccinations. By controlling exposure and ensuring vaccination, your pet should be safe from these potentially devastating diseases.

It is beyond the scope of this book to settle all the controversies of vaccination, but they are worth mentioning. Should vaccines be combined in a single injection? It's convenient and cheaper to do it this way, but might some vaccine ingredients interfere with others? Some say yes, some say no. Are vaccine schedules designed for convenience or effectiveness? Mostly convenience. Some ingredients may only need to be given every two or more years, but research is incomplete. Should the dose of the vaccine vary with weight, or should a Labrador Retriever receive the same dose as a Chihuahua and Great Dane? Good questions, no definitive answers. Finally, should we be using modified-live or inactivated vaccine products? There is no short answer for this debate. Ask your veterinarian, and do a lot of reading yourself!

CANINE COUGH

Canine infectious tracheobronchitis, also known as canine cough and kennel cough, is a contagious viral/bacterial disease that results in a hacking cough that may persist for many weeks. It is common wherever dogs are kept in close quarters, such as kennels, grooming parlors, dog shows, training classes, and even veterinary clinics. The condition doesn't respond well to most medications, but eventually clears spontaneously over the course of many weeks. Pneumonia is a possible but uncommon complication.

Prevention is best achieved by limiting your dog's exposure and having it vaccinated. The fewer opportunities you give your dog to come in contact with others, the less the likelihood of getting infected. Vaccination is not foolproof because many different viruses can be involved. Parainfluenza virus is included in most vaccines and is one of the more common viruses known to initiate the condition. *Bordetella bronchiseptica* is the bacterium most often associated with tracheobronchitis, and a vaccine for this is now available. This vaccine is squirted into the dog's nostrils to help stop the infection before it gets deeper into the respiratory tract, and it needs to be repeated twice yearly for dogs at risk. Make sure the vaccination is given several days (preferably two weeks) before exposure to ensure maximum protection.

Today's vaccines are extremely effective, and properly vaccinated dogs are at minimal risk of contracting viral infections.

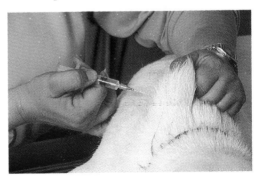

FIRST AID

by Judy Iby, RVT

**KNOWING YOUR DOG
IN GOOD HEALTH**

With some experience, you will learn how to give your dog a physical at home, and consequently will learn to recognize many potential problems. If you can detect a problem early, you can seek timely medical help and thereby decrease your  dog's risk of developing a more serious problem.

Facing page: For the safety of your Labrador, it is important to know first aid techniques to be able to save his life in an emergency.

Every pet owner should be able to take his pet's temperature, pulse, respirations, and check the capillary refill time (CRT). Knowing what is normal will alert the pet owner to what is abnormal, and this can be life saving for the sick pet.

TEMPERATURE

The dog's normal temperature is 100.5 to 102.5 degrees Fahrenheit. Take the temperature rectally for at least one minute. Be sure to shake the thermometer down first, and you may find it helpful to lubricate the end. It is easy to take the temperature with the dog in a standing position. Be sure to hold on to the thermometer so that it isn't expelled or sucked in. A dog

It is easy to take your Labrador's temperature with the dog in a standing position. Be sure to hold on to the thermometer so that it isn't expelled or sucked in.

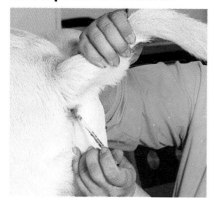

could have an elevated temperature if he is excited or if he is overheated; however, a high temperature could indicate a medical emergency. On the other hand, if the temperature is below 100 degrees, this could also indicate an emergency.

CAPILLARY REFILL TIME AND GUM COLOR

It is important to know how your dog's gums look when he is healthy, so you will be able to recognize a difference if he is not feeling well. There are a few breeds, among them the Chow Chow and its relatives, that have black gums and a black tongue. This is normal for them. In general, a healthy dog will have bright pink gums. Pale gums are an indication of shock or anemia and are an emergency. Likewise, any yellowish tint is an indication of a sick dog. To check capillary refill time (CRT) press your thumb against the dog's gum. The gum will blanch out (turn white) but should refill (return to the normal pink color) in one to two seconds. CRT is very important. If the refill time is slow and your dog is acting poorly, you should call your veterinarian immediately.

HEART RATE, PULSE, AND RESPIRATIONS

Heart rate depends on the breed of the dog and his health. Normal heart rates range from about 50 beats per minute in the larger breeds to 130 beats per minute in the smaller breeds. You can take the heart rate by pressing your fingertips on the dog's chest. Count for either 10 or 15 seconds, and then multiply by either 6 or 4 to obtain the rate per minute. A normal pulse is the same as the heart rate and is taken at the femoral artery located on the insides of both rear legs. Respirations should be observed and depending on the size and breed of the dog should be 10 to 30 per minute. Obviously, illness or excitement could account for abnormal rates.

This vet is listening to the dog's heart through a stethoscope; however, you should learn how to find your Labrador's pulse at home.

PREPARING FOR AN EMERGENCY

It is a good idea to prepare for an emergency by making a list and keeping it by the phone. This list should include:

1. Your veterinarian's name, address, phone number, and office hours.
2. Your veterinarian's policy for after-hour care. Does he take his own emergencies or does he refer them to an emergency clinic?
3. The name, address, phone number and hours of the emergency clinic your veterinarian uses.
4. The number of the National Poison Control Center for Animals in Illinois: 1-800-548-2423. It is open 24 hours a day.

In a true emergency, time is of the essence. Some signs of an emergency may be:

1. Pale gums or an abnormal heart rate.
2. Abnormal temperature, lower than 100 degrees or over 104 degrees.
3. Shock or lethargy.
4. Spinal paralysis.

A dog hit by car needs to be checked out and probably should have radiographs of the chest and abdomen to rule out pneumothorax or ruptured bladder.

EMERGENCY MUZZLE

An injured, frightened dog may not even recognize his owner and may be inclined to bite. If your dog should be injured, you may need to muzzle him to protect yourself before you try to handle him. It is a good idea to practice muzzling the calm, healthy dog so you understand the technique. Slip a lead over his head for control. You can tie his mouth shut with something like a two-foot-long bandage or piece of cloth. A necktie, stocking, leash or even a piece of rope will also work.

1. Make a large loop by tying a loose knot in the middle of the bandage or cloth.
2. Hold the ends up, one in each hand.
3. Slip the loop over the dog's muzzle and lower jaw, just behind his nose.
4. Quickly tighten the loop so he can't open his mouth.
5. Tie the ends under his lower jaw.
6. Make a knot there and pull the ends back on each side of his face, under the ears, to the back of his head.

If he should start to vomit, you will need to remove the muzzle immediately.

ANTIFREEZE POISONING

Antifreeze in the driveway is a potential killer. Because antifreeze is sweet, dogs will lap it up. The active ingredient in antifreeze is ethylene glycol, which causes irreversible kidney damage. If you witness your pet ingesting antifreeze, you should call your veterinarian immediately. He may recommend that you induce vomiting at once by using hydrogen peroxide, or he may recommend a test to confirm antifreeze ingestion. Treatment is aggressive and must be administered promptly if the dog is to live, but you wouldn't want to subject your dog to unnecessary treatment.

BEE STINGS

A severe reaction to a bee sting (anaphylaxis) can result in difficulty breathing, collapse and even death. A symptom of a bee sting is swelling around the muzzle and face. Bee stings are antihistamine responsive. Over-the-counter antihistamines are available. Ask your veterinarian for recommendations on safe antihistamines to use and the doses to administer. You should monitor the dog's gum color and respirations and watch for a decrease in swelling. If your dog is showing signs of anaphylaxis, your veterinarian may need to give him an injection of corticosteroids. It would be wise to call your veterinarian and confirm treatment.

BLEEDING

Bleeding can occur in many forms, such as a ripped dewclaw, a toenail cut too short, a puncture wound, a severe laceration, etc. If a pressure bandage is needed, it must be released every 15–20 minutes. Be careful of elastic bandages since it is easy to apply them too tightly. Any bandage material should be clean. If no regular bandage is available, a small towel or wash cloth can be used to cover the wound and bind it with a necktie, scarf, or something similar. Styptic powder, or even a soft cake of soap, can be used to stop a bleeding toenail. A ripped dewclaw or toenail may need to be cut back by the veterinarian and possibly treated with antibiotics. Depending on their severity, lacerations and puncture wounds may also need professional treatment. Your first thought should be to clean the wound with peroxide, soap and water, or some other antiseptic cleanser. Don't use alcohol since

it deters the healing of the tissue.

BLOAT

Although not generally considered a first aid situation, bloat can occur in a dog rather suddenly. Truly, it is an emergency! Gastric dilatation-volvulus or gastric torsion—the twisting of the stomach to cut off both entry and exit, causing the organ to "bloat," is a disorder primarily found in the larger, more deep-chested breeds. It is life threatening and requires immediate veterinary assistance.

BURNS

If your dog gets a chemical burn, call your veterinarian immediately. Rinse any other burns with cold water and if the burn is significant, call your veterinarian. It may be necessary to clip the hair around the burn so it will be easier to keep clean. You can cleanse the wound on a daily basis with saline and apply a topical antimicrobial ointment, such as silver sulfadiazine 1 percent cream or gentamicin cream. Burns can be debilitating, especially to an older pet. They can cause pain and shock. It takes about three weeks for the skin to slough after the burn and there is the possibility of permanent hair loss.

CARDIOPULMONARY RESUSCITATION (CPR)

Check to see if your dog has a heart beat, pulse and spontaneous respiration. If his pupils are already dilated and fixed, the prognosis is less favorable. This is an emergency situation that requires two people to administer lifesaving techniques. One person needs to breathe for the dog while the other person tries to establish heart rhythm. Mouth to mouth resuscitation starts with two initial breaths, one to one and a half seconds in duration. After the initial breaths, breathe for the dog once after every five chest compressions. (You do not want to expand the dog's lungs while his chest is being compressed.) You inhale, cover the dog's nose with your mouth, and exhale *gently*. You should see the dog's chest expand. Sometimes, pulling the tongue forward stimulates respiration. You should be ventilating the dog 12–20 times per minute. The person managing the chest compressions should have the dog lying on his right side with one hand on either side of the dog's chest, directed over the heart between the fourth and fifth ribs (usually this is the point of the flexed elbow). The number of compressions administered depends on the size of the patient. Attempt 80–120 compressions per minute. Check for spontaneous respiration and/or heart beat. If present, monitor the patient and discontinue resuscitation. If you haven't already done so, call your veterinarian at once and make arrangements to take your pet in for professional treatment.

CHOCOLATE TOXICOSIS

Dogs like chocolate, but chocolate kills dogs. Its two basic chemicals, caffeine and theobromine, overstimulate the dog's nervous system. Ten ounces of milk chocolate can kill a 12-pound dog. Symptoms of poisoning include restlessness, vomiting, increased heart rate, seizure, and coma. Death is possible. If your dog has ingested chocolate, you can give syrup of ipecac at a dosage of one-eighth of a teaspoon per pound to induce vomiting. Two tablespoons of hydrogen peroxide is an alternative treatment.

CHOKING

You need to open the dog's mouth to see if any object is visible. Try to hold him upside down to see if the object can be dislodged. While you are working on your dog, call your veterinarian, as time may be critical.

DOG BITES

If your dog is bitten, wash the area and determine the severity of the situation. Some bites may need immediate attention, for instance, if it is bleeding profusely or if a lung is punctured. Other bites may be only superficial scrapes. Most dog bite cases need to be seen by the veterinarian, and some may require antibiotics. It is important that you learn if the offending dog has had a rabies vaccination. This is important for your dog, but also for you, in case you are the victim. Wash the wound and call your doctor for further instructions. You should check on your tetanus vaccination history.

Rarely, and I mean rarely, do dogs get tetanus. If the offending dog is a stray, try to confine him for observation. He will need to be confined for ten days. A dog that has bitten a human and is not current on his rabies vaccination cannot receive a rabies vaccination for ten days. Dog bites should be reported to the Board of Health.

DROWNING

Remove any debris from the dog's mouth and swing the dog, holding him upside down. Stimulate respiration by pulling his tongue forward. Administer CPR if necessary, and call your veterinarian. Don't give up work-

If you let your Labrador Retriever swim in your swimming pool, make sure you show him how to get out. Never leave your dog unattended in a swimming area!

ing on the dog. Be sure to wrap him in blankets if he is cold or in shock.

ELECTROCUTION

You may want to look into puppy proofing your house by installing GFCIs (Ground Fault Circuit Interrupters) on your electrical outlets. A GFCI just saved my dog's life. He had pulled an extension cord into his crate and was "teething" on it at seven years of age. The GFCI kept him from being electrocuted. Turn off the current before touching the dog. Resuscitate him by administering CPR and pulling his tongue forward to stimulate respiration. Try mouth-to-mouth breathing if the dog is not breathing. Take him to your veterinarian as soon as possible since electrocution can cause internal problems, such as lung damage, which need medical treatment.

EYES

Red eyes indicate inflammation, and any redness to the upper white part of the eye (sclera) may constitute an emergency. Squinting, cloudiness to the cornea, or loss of vision could indicate severe problems, such as glaucoma, anterior uveitis and episcleritis. Glaucoma is an emergency if you want to save

the dog's eye. A prolapsed third eyelid is abnormal and is a symptom of an underlying problem. If something should get in your dog's eye, flush it out with cold water or a saline eye wash. Epiphora and allergic conjunctivitis are annoying and frequently persistent problems. Epiphora (excessive tearing) leaves the area below the eye wet and sometimes stained. The wetness may lead to a bacterial infection. There are numerous causes (allergies, infections, foreign matter, abnormally located eyelashes and adjacent facial hair that rubs against the eyeball, defects or diseases of the tear drainage system, birth defects of the eyelids, etc.) and the treatment is based on the cause. Keeping the hair around the eye cut short and sponging the eye daily will give relief. Many cases are responsive to medical treatment. Allergic conjunctivitis may be a seasonal problem if the dog has inhalant allergies (e.g., ragweed), or it may be a year 'round problem. The conjunctiva becomes red and swollen and is prone to a bacterial infection associated with mucus accumulation or pus in the eye. Again, keeping the hair around the eyes short will give relief. Mild corticosteroid drops or ointment will

Labradors will eat anything! Always supervise your puppy and don't allow him to chew on anything but safe chew devices designed for just that purpose—tennis balls don't fit the bill.

also give relief. The underlying problem should be investigated.

FISH HOOKS

An imbedded fish hook will probably need to be removed by the veterinarian. More than likely, sedation will be required along with antibiotics. Don't try to remove it yourself. The shank of the hook will need to be cut off in order to push the other end through.

FOREIGN OBJECTS

I can't tell you how many chicken bones my first dog ingested. Fortunately she had a "cast iron stomach" and never suffered the consequences. However, she was always going to the veterinarian for treatment. Not all dogs are so lucky. It is unbelievable what some dogs will take a liking to. I have assisted in surgeries in which all kinds of foreign objects were removed from the stomach and/or intestinal tract. Those objects included socks, pantyhose, stockings, clothing, diapers, sanitary products, plastic, toys, and, last but not least, rawhides. Surgery is costly and not always successful, especially if it is performed too late. If you see or suspect your dog has ingested a foreign object, contact your veterinarian immediately. He may tell you to induce vomiting or he may have you bring your dog to the clinic immediately. Don't induce vomiting without the veterinarian's permission, since the object may cause more damage on the way back up than it would if you allow it to pass through.

HEATSTROKE

Heatstroke is an emergency! The classic signs are rapid, shallow breathing; rapid heartbeat; a temperature above 104 degrees; and subsequent collapse. The dog needs to be cooled as quickly as possible and treated immediately by the veterinarian. If possible, spray him down with cool water and pack ice around his head, neck, and groin. Monitor his temperature and stop the cooling process as soon as his temperature reaches 103 degrees. Nevertheless, you will need to keep monitoring his temperature to be sure it doesn't elevate again. If the temperature continues to drop to below 100 degrees, it could be life threatening. Get professional help immediately. Prevention is more successful than treatment. Those at the greatest risk are brachycephalic (short nosed) breeds, obese dogs, and those that suffer from cardiovascular disease. Dogs are not able to cool off by sweating as people can. Their only way is through panting and radiation of heat from the skin surface. When stressed and exposed to high environmental temperature, high humidity, and poor ventilation, a dog can suffer heatstroke very quickly. Many people do not realize how quickly a car can overheat. Never leave a dog unattended in a car. It is even against the law in some states. Also, a brachycephalic, obese, or infirm dog should never be left unattended outside during inclement weather and should have his activities curtailed. Any dog left outside, by law, must be assured adequate shelter (including shade) and fresh water.

POISONS

Try to locate the source of the poison (the container which lists the ingredients) and call your veterinarian immediately. Be prepared to give the age and weight of your dog, the quantity of poison consumed and the probable time of ingestion. Your veterinarian will want you to read off the ingredients. If you can't reach him, you can call a local poison center or the National Poison Control Center for Animals in Illinois, which is open

24 hours a day. Their phone number is 1-800-548-2423. There is a charge for their service, so you may need to have a credit card number available.

Symptoms of poisoning include muscle trembling and weakness, increased salivation, vomiting and loss of bowel control. There are numerous household toxins (over 500,000). A dog can be poisoned by toxins in the garbage. Other poisons include pesticides, pain relievers, prescription drugs, plants, chocolate, and cleansers. Since I own small dogs I don't have to worry about my dogs jumping up to the kitchen counters, but when I owned a large breed she would clean the counter, eating all the prescription medications.

Your pet can be poisoned by means other than directly ingesting the toxin. Ingesting a rodent that has ingested a rodenticide is one example. It is possible for a dog to have a reaction to the pesticides used by exterminators. If this is suspected you should contact the exterminator about the potential dangers of the pesticides used and their side effects.

Don't give human drugs to your dog unless your veterinarian has given his approval. Some human medications can be deadly to dogs.

POISONOUS PLANTS

Amaryllis (bulb)	Jasmine (berries)
Andromeda	Jerusalem Cherry
Apple Seeds (cyanide)	Jimson Weed
Arrowgrass	Laburnum
Avocado	Larkspur
Azalea	Laurel
Bittersweet	Locoweed
Boxwood	Marigold
Buttercup	Marijuana
Caladium	Mistletoe (berries)
Castor Bean	Monkshood
Cherry Pits	Mushrooms
Chokecherry	Narcissus (bulb)
Climbing Lily	Nightshade
Crown of Thorns	Oleander
Daffodil (bulb)	Peach
Daphne	Philodendron
Delphinium	Poison Ivy
Dieffenbachia	Privet
Dumb Cane	Rhododendron
Elderberry	Rhubarb
Elephant Ear	Snow on the Mountain
English Ivy	Stinging Nettle
Foxglove	Toadstool
Hemlock	Tobacco
Holly	Tulip (bulb)
Hyacinth (bulb)	Walnut
Hydrangea	Wisteria
Iris (bulb)	Yew
Japanese Yew	

This list was published in the American Kennel Club *Gazette*, February, 1995. As the list states these are common poisonous plants, but this list may not be complete. If your dog ingests a poisonous plant, try to identify it and call your veterinarian. Some plants cause more harm than others.

PORCUPINE QUILLS

Removal of quills is best left up to your veterinarian since it can be quite painful. Your unhappy dog would probably appreciate being sedated for the removal of the quills.

SEIZURE (CONVULSION OR FIT)

Many breeds, including mixed breeds, are predisposed to seizures, although a seizure may be secondary to an underlying medical condition. Usually a seizure is not considered an emergency unless it lasts longer than ten minutes. Nevertheless, you should notify your veterinarian. Dogs do not swallow their tongues. Do not handle the dog's mouth since your dog probably cannot control his actions and may inadvertently bite you. The seizure can be mild; for instance, a dog can have a seizure standing up. More frequently the dog will lose consciousness and may urinate and/or defecate. The best thing you can do for your dog is to put him in a safe place or to block off the stairs or areas where he can fall.

SEVERE TRAUMA

See that the dog's head and neck are extended so if the dog is unconscious or in shock, he is able to breathe. If there is any vomitus, you should try to get the head extended down with the body elevated to prevent vomitus from being aspirated. Alert your veterinarian that you are on your way.

SHOCK

Shock is a life threatening condition and requires immediate veterinary care. It can occur after an injury or even after severe fright. Other causes of shock are hemorrhage, fluid loss, sepsis, toxins, adrenal insufficiency, cardiac failure, and anaphylaxis. The symptoms are a rapid weak pulse, shallow breathing, dilated pupils, subnormal temperature, and muscle weakness. The capillary refill time (CRT) is slow, taking longer than two seconds for normal gum color to return. Keep the dog warm while transporting him to the veterinary clinic. Time is critical for survival.

SKUNKS

Skunk spraying is not necessarily an emergency, although it would be in my house. If the dog's eyes are sprayed, you need to rinse them well with water. One remedy for deskunking the dog is to wash him in tomato juice and follow with a soap and water bath. The newest remedy is bathing the dog in a mixture of one quart of three percent hydrogen peroxide, quarter cup baking soda, and one teaspoon liquid soap. Rinse well. There are also commercial products available.

SNAKE BITES

It is always a good idea to know what poisonous snakes reside in your area. Rattlesnakes, water moccasins, copperheads, and coral snakes are residents of some areas of the United States. Pack ice around the area that is bitten and call your veterinarian immediately to alert him that you are on your way. Try to identify the snake or at least be able to describe it (for the use of antivenin). It is possible that he may send you to another clinic that has the proper antivenin.

Working Labrador Retrievers are at more of a risk of encountering hazardous critters such as porcupines, snakes, toads, and skunks. It is important to be aware of these dangers when you are in the field.

TOAD POISONING

Bufo toads are quite deadly. You should find out if these nasty little critters are native to your area.

VACCINATION REACTION

Once in a while, a dog may suffer an anaphylactic reaction to a vaccine. Symptoms include swelling around the muzzle, extending to the eyes. Your veterinarian may ask you to return to his office to determine the severity of the reaction. It is possible that your dog may need to stay at the hospital for a few hours during future vaccinations.

RECOMMENDED READING

THE OFFICIAL BOOK OF THE LABRADOR RETRIEVER

by The Labrador Retriever Club, Inc.
TS-241, 448 pages
Over 200 full-color photographs

The Labrador Retriever Club, Inc., established in 1931, endures as the proud protector and parent club for the Labrador Retriever in the United States. T.F.H. Publications, Inc. is pleased to join forces with this highly regarded breed club to produce *The Official Book of the Labrador Retriever.* This is an entire library of excellent information in one timeless book illustrated with hundreds of beautiful photographs of the most important Labrador Retrievers of all time.

THE BOOK OF THE LABRADOR RETRIEVER

by Anna Katherine Nicholas
H-1059, 480 pages
Over 100 full-color photographs

The Book of the Labrador Retriever is a most ambitious work about the breed. Labrador history and husbandry are covered in exacting detail, highlighted by beautiful photographic coverage of Labradors and Labrador owners of today and yesterday.

THE PROPER CARE OF LABRADOR RETRIEVERS

by Dennis and Pat Livesey
TW-140, 256 pages
Over 200 full-color photos

Written with remarkable clarity and illustrated throughout with full-color photos of top-notch breed representatives, *The Proper Care of Labrador Retrievers* covers all the basics of Labrador ownership, from selecting the ideal puppy to keeping adults vibrant and healthy throughout their lives.

OWNER'S GUIDE TO DOG HEALTH

TS-214, 432 pages
Over 300 color photographs

Winner of the 1995 Dog Writers Association of America's Best Health Book, this comprehensive title gives accurate, up-to-date information on all the major disorders and conditions found in dogs. Completely illustrated to help owners visualize signs of illness, different states of infection, procedures and treatment, it covers nutrition, skin disorders, disorders of the major body systems (reproductive, digestive, respiratory), eye problems, vaccines and vaccinations, dental health and more.